Presence

Family Worship
In Your Home

Taking up God's generational call for the
Family Altar

Alicia White

𝒞hosen 𝒮tones Minsitries

www.chosenstones.org

Presence-Driven Family Worship
Copyright © 2016 by Alicia White
Published by Chosen Stones Ministries
Email: info@ChosenStones.org
Web: www.chosenstones.org
Call: 513-779-2822

Unless noted, all scripture is from the New King James Version of the Holy Bible

This book is lovingly dedicated to my family

My first and most important calling is to my own family. I have failed many of times but there is no love like family love. My kids and husband have always had my back, they have been my greatest encourager, and been patient with me when I have had my head in the computer trying to get down on paper all that is in my heart. Balancing ministry to families with ministry to my own family has always been a challenge and I pray one I never stop meeting. I love the gift God has given me in my family and treasure knowing that what God has begun in us He will see it to its completion in the generations to come. My greatest success in life will always be measured by how much I have loved and poured into my family.

CONTENTS

About the Author

I wanted to start off by sharing a bit about my own testimony as a parent. Even though I was raised up around the church and the things of God, due to the tragic loss of my own father at four years old, my family life became broken. My mother, who I love and respect dearly, at the time, was a young twenty seven year old widow with two little girls; my sister being six, and me four. She did the best with what she knew how to do, but unfortunately it lead us down the road of living a much separate family life than what we knew in church. Today my mother and step Father love the Lord very much and I could not be prouder of them.

Even despite the culture and family life I was raised in that was confusing and compromising, as I child, I knew my Daddy God was there and I had conversations with Him frequently. I stayed close to Him until I hit my teen years. But without the foundations of a Christian home life to stand on, I drifted away from the Lord for eight years. During that time away from the Lord I met my high school sweetheart, Jason, who did not know the Lord at all. We married and began to start a life with each other.

Neither I nor my husband walked with the Lord as we started our family. But God was soon to change that. When our first child, our only son, was two, I found myself struggling with keeping a viable pregnancy. After my second miscarriage, I was desperate for God's love and presence again and returned back to him. Within the first couple of months of finding a church and relationship with Jesus again, I got pregnant for the third time since our son was born. And again an early ultrasound detected that I was going to lose this child too. With the flu and a 104 temperature, our newly found pastor came over and prayed for me. The next week another ultrasound testified to a miracle of a healthy little girl we soon named Faithanna. Our season of emotional trauma was not yet over though. Faithanna was born with a kidney disease that took one of her kidneys from her. Eight months after having Faithanna I then got pregnant with twins, one of which I lost. The precious little girl that survived we named Hope. And to add to the top of this incredible time of trials and tribulations, Jason got laid off from his job during 911 and was unemployed for eighteen months.

The revelation that came out of that incredible time of battle though is what made us into the parents we are today. Jason received Christ while I was pregnant with Faithanna, and as we together, began to walk down the road that was set before us, we realized that God was doing something incredible in us every step of the way. We found ourselves with a deep revelation that having children is a miracle and a precious gift from God not to be taken for granted. There was a deep knowing in our Spirit that God had chosen us to be the parents of our children, and that He was beckoning us to be a part of something bigger than ourselves in this role. We knew that if we desired for our family to take a different path then perhaps our childhoods had taken us, it would require from us radical change and intentional effort.

We began to evaluate what we desired for our children and for our family; what things mattered the most at the end of the day. We set out to do things differently, but most importantly Biblically. God wasn't just going to be a part of our family life, but our life. As we fell madly in the love with God and His presence, and made that our lifestyle, our children naturally followed. We didn't have to force them or even entice them. Just as Jesus saw and did what His Father was doing, they saw what daddy (and mommy) did and that became the normal culture for them. The family altar was established in our family by creating a lifestyle of His presence.

The Lord eventually gifted us with one more child, who I affectionately call my "grace" child because I had no complication carrying her whatsoever. Her name is Isabella Grace. As I finish writing this book we are preparing to send out our first and only son off to college to study ministry. Our three girls underneath him are fourteen, thirteen, and six. I can say, only by the grace of God and our willingness to intentionally go after His presence in our family, they all don't just love the Lord but are passionately pursing Him in a lifestyle of worship. Their hearts are not intertwined with the world, but it is clear what they make their life and priority; God's presence and will in every way.

Through the years, the Lord has used us to share His heart for His children and families in both Children's Ministry and Youth Ministry, and now through our own family ministry called Chosen Stones. I am also currently the Ohio Director for Kids in Ministry int., which is foundered and directed by Becky Fischer in North Dakota. I am honored and excited with anticipation to partner with God to see a whole generation of families bring the altar back into their homes causing authentic transformation in their families, in our churches, and the culture around us.

Our Daughter, Hope, under the power and presence of the Jesus in a revival service.

Our Daughter, Faithanna, Interceding under the anointing and presence of Jesus in one of our family gatherings.

Our son, Samuel, preaching at a youth service

Our 6 year old daughter, Isabella, by herself in deep worship in a family gathering

Forwards

Pastor Barry Clardy, Senior Pastor of Princeton Pike Church of God

There is nothing that God created with more value than the gift of the family. In fact, He created the family before he created His church. Alicia White has captured in this book the very heart of God concerning the dynamic of family worship welded with wisdom & insight on understanding the call to worship as a family. The valuable treasures within this book will revolutionize your understanding of the privilege, power, & potential that results from practicing your faith in Christ within the frame work of your family. Your life & family will never be the same as you open up your heart to the profound & practical teachings of this book.

The investment of each chapter sown into your life will without doubt bring a fruitful harvest to you & your family. Enjoy!

Becky Fischer, Kids in Ministry international

Without a doubt, one of the toughest jobs anyone can tackle is that of parenting. But it's especially challenging for Christian parents who want to raise their children to be ardent, devoted followers of Christ. There was a time in our history when all it took to produce good Christian kids, was to have a good Christian family environment, parents who loved the Lord, prayer over meals, and bedtime, and who all attended church together each week.

The local church was the center of our social lives then, and Sunday School was highly attended. Even the educational systems and whole culture basically supported a Christian worldview.

Those were the days when no one challenged hanging the Ten Commandments on the walls of our government buildings, nor debated whether or not we should put "In God We Trust" on our money. There was no Internet, social media, and Disney was still a highly rated, safe, trusted source of family entertainment. Kids never got expelled from school because they prayed over their lunch, and other religions, like Islam, were not more celebrated than Christianity.

But those days are over, and like it or not, they aren't coming back any time soon. So while we may grieve a simpler time in history, we have to face reality that people in many other nations have faced for decades. The truth is, if we are going to raise spiritual champions it's not going to happen by accident. It's going to be the result of deliberate, on purpose, goal oriented, focused godly parenting. The ramifications of not doing so are enormous, not just in our own lives, but in our culture.

But many Christians did not come from homes where godly parenting was modeled. Many of us have never been told how to do it or what it is supposed to look like. The majority of them are left to figure it out for themselves. Almost nothing is said from the pulpit to give us direction. No manuals are handed out when people get saved that instruct them how to disciple their own children. The most parents have known to do is to take their kids to church every Sunday—but those days are gone too, even for the most faithful.

Some parents have reasoned that placing their children in good Christian schools, even though it means financial hardship and sacrifice, was the right answer. But tragically, research has shown many times they are no better, and sometimes worse, at passing on Christian faith than public schools are. The reason is they are desperate to survive financially, so they naturally open their arms to people of all levels of Christianity. Then, so as not to offend anyone, they dramatically water down any Christian influence they may have had at one time.

Still other Christian parents choose to homeschool their kids. But that is not necessarily the answer either. If they are not simultaneously adding deliberate, well-planned, spiritual teaching to their daily lives, just isolating their kids from the outside world does not equal godly parenting and a Christian upbringing.

Because of their own spiritual insecurities, many parents do not feel qualified to teach their children about God and a Christian ethos. They struggle many times with understanding scripture themselves, much less, scaling down heavy concepts to teach their young children. So too often, they do nothing and hope for the best.

But that is the worst thing that a Christian parent should do. By the grace of God, there is a way to do this. After all, in Deuteronomy 6, God commanded His people to diligently teach their children to love and know the Word of God. He would not have told us to do something that was impossible to do. Many scriptures declare we're to teach our children and pass our faith on to the next generation.

If you are a parent who has struggled with how to disciple your child, today there are many books, videos, and other materials to help. With such a plethora of resources now available, there is really no reason parents cannot get the tools and advice they need to develop a love for God in the hearts of their children.

You are holding one valuable resource in your hands. It is short. It is simple. But it is a great launching pad that will start you in the right direction. Once you go through this beginning stage, you will be better prepared to go on from here. Once you begin to see fruit in the lives of your children, hopefully you will be motivated to seek out more resources and more help.

Alicia writes from personal experience and knows the fruit of making a deliberate effort to disciple her children. I encourage you to follow her model to get you started.

Introduction

It is time for a Selah moment.

Between going to work, soccer games, football practices, school work, school events, and trying to squeeze in a family vacation, have you ever paused long enough to ask God if you were doing all that He wants you to do as a parent? Sometimes it feels like we are just too exhausted to add another thing to our plate. But, what if the things on our plate are actually keeping us from the one thing we should be doing as a parent? Perhaps a better question to ask God is, "Am I too busy doing good things that I have no time to do God things?"

As parents, often day after day we try to just "get through" and "maintain" in a world of craziness. But in so doing we miss the bigger picture of why God called us to be parents and raise a family. You see according Jeremiah 1:5, God knew your children before they were conceived; He knew His calling and plans for them; He knew when they were going to be born, and most of all, to whom they were going to be born to. He chose you to be their parent for such as time as this. It is not by happenstance. God entrusted you with His child and is simply waiting for you to ask Him what He desires you to do to help raise them. Your position of a parent is a calling of God with a purpose much bigger and greater than you.

God is a generational God. He can see the end from the beginning. His ways and thoughts are bigger than ours, and His perspective goes far beyond the moment, the day, the year, and even seasons. In the tug and pull of our fast paced culture, could it be that we are running right past the greatest calling God will ever give us in our lifetime because we simply have not laid hold of His generational vision for our family? Are we failing to rise to the call of parenting at the fullest potential God has for us? Could we be missing the forest for the trees?

Think about the word "calling." A calling according to the Webster dictionary "is a strong inner impulse towards a particular course of action, especially when accompanied by conviction or divine influence." A calling of God is an inner conviction to intentionally move in a certain direction or action. It is a divinely- inspired thought or position that drives us into action; a predestined anointing to accomplish a particular task for Him. It is a position or place of office that supersedes any other in the natural. The word "calling" holds a heavy weight that denotes a purpose without question. Most of us look at a pastor or an evangelist as having a calling. Some even see a doctor, teacher, or nurse as having a calling. But few ever think of mom or dad as a calling. Be honest, if someone came up to you and asked you what you were called to do for God, would the first answer out of your mouth be a "mom" or "dad?" However, as you will see within the pages of this book, parenting is the single most important calling you will ever have from God and it should be the first answer out of our mouth.

Why is it that we do not equate parenting with a calling? I believe the answer lies in our inability to have a vision for our role as parents. A person's measure of success within their calling is directly related to how well they perceive and lay hold of the vision set before them. It is a matter of taking ownership of the vision and allowing it to drive you to do whatever you have to do to see it come to pass. God never calls anyone to something that He has not first given them a vision for. He says in Proverbs 29:18, "Where there is no vision, the people perish: but he that keepeth the law, happy is he (KJV)." Laying hold of God's vision is crucial for any calling He has for you. It is equally important to even our own happiness as a mother or father.

God told Noah what was going to happen on earth before He called Him to build the ark. He cast vision to Moses, of freeing His people, before He called Him to be the liberator. We can look at Mary, the most honored parent of humanity, as another example. Mary was told, in Luke 1:31-33,"And behold, you will conceive in your womb and bring forth a Son, and shall call His name Jesus. He will be great, and will be called the Son of the Highest; and the Lord God will give Him the throne of His father David and He will reign over the house of Jacob forever, and of His kingdom there will be no end." God cast vision to Mary so that she would lay hold of her calling; to be the mother of the child who would transform the earth forever. Mary's answer to this casting of vision was, "Behold the maidservant of the Lord! Let it be to me according to your word (Luke 1:38)." God counted her worthy to entrust her with His child, and she arose to the occasion with a resounding YES! The same goes for you and me.

No, we are not the parents of Jesus, but if we can lay hold of the truth that we too are parents entrusted with God's child who has the potential to be a world changer, we will fulfill the high calling of parenting.

We have but a short time to run with this calling called parenting. We may be parents for a lifetime, but we do not have a lifetime to raise and disciple our children for the Lord. We must slow down long enough to lay hold of God's vision for our children and family. It must be the driving force in everything we do as parents. If not, we will run this race called "raising a family" never seeing our full Godly potential as parents nor the potential of our children come to past. We will look back and lament about how quickly the time passed, full of regrets and should of's, only to find out God's purposes through our family will perish with us because we failed to capture His vision.

"Presence-Driven Family Worship" is about a call back to the ancient ways; the ancient vision that God established for families. God's heart for families always was to create a perpetual generation of family worshippers that would daily abide in His presence. However, today, more often than not, our children go one way at church and we go the other. The same thing is daily occurring in our homes. God's ancient vision of a family altar, that inhabits the presence of Jesus, is almost non-existent. Satan has used busyness, cultural ideologies, and every distraction at his disposal to keep our families from making

Jesus the center of our homes. He has robbed us of presence-filled family worship. The altar of our home, where God's vision for our families is to be cultivated and manifested, has been stripped away and replaced with busyness, rebellion, compromise, distractions, and selfish lusts of the flesh. It is time to take the vision back and lay hold of the compass that points us to the family altar once again.

Satan understands the powerful gift and weapon we cradle in our hands called our children, and He is battling for their souls, and the destruction of our family inheritance. The family altar was created to be that place where God fights for us, a spiritual battle that must be fought in the spirit. As parents, entrusted with God's children, we can't afford to busy ourselves doing "good" things and not "God" things. It is the purpose of this book to cultivate a generation of families who will bring the altar and vision of God back once again in their homes, and create an atmosphere for the habituation of the presence of God.

We must fill our homes with the Holy Spirit and allow Him to have His way with our family. We must regenerate a perpetual generation of worshippers that allows God's vision and presence to direct them in everything they do and say. We need more than self-help books and the wisdom of man for our families; we need the power of the Holy Spirit that can do more in one minute than a lifetime of Christian counseling can do. Jesus said that the Holy Spirit would come and lead us into all truth and give us the power to defeat our enemy who seeks to destroy us...this is the kind of help that our families need today.

In this book, I will take you from the bigger picture of God's generational vision for families, to His calling in us as parents, to a Biblical blueprint for family worship and ministry, and finally a step by step instruction manual found in God's word for presence-driven family worship called the tabernacle of Moses. But this isn't just another book with good information. I also provide you with very practical, creative, and spirit-filled ways that you can begin and continue in the vision and calling of the family altar through what I call "jumping off" ideas.

I have including some very powerful testimonies of my own family in very strategic places, but have intentionally not allowed this book to become a "journal", if you will, of our family's encounters and experiences with the Lord in family worship. I know how we can be as parents; we can easily allow the Holy Spirit to use other's experiences as a way for us to compare and find fault in our own family. The Spirit of condemnation is such a strong hold in parents today that I literally felt the Lord cautioning me to not make room for comparisons, condemnation, or even pressure to perform, through too many personal testimonies. The Holy Spirit impressed upon me that He wanted everyone that reads this book to find a clean canvas, and allow the Holy Spirit to begin to paint the story of their own family's encounters and experiences in presence-driven family worship. Every family is different; every family will have a story. It's time to create your own family's history book with God that will ensure your generation to the next will worship the Lord.

Will you accept the call to presence-driven family worship!

First Half

God's Vision for our Families

God's Generational Vision

Chapter 1

Multiply the Kingdom

"So God created man in His own image; in the image of God He created him; male and female He created them. Then God blessed them, and God said to them, "Be fruitful and multiply; fill the earth and subdue it; have dominion over the fish of the sea, over the birds of the air, and over every living thing that moves on the earth." Genesis 1:27-28

We must start out on this journey of presence-driven family worship by addressing God's vision for families; why He established them and what our goal should be as Christ-following parents as we shape and endeavor to grow our children up in the fear and ways of the Lord.

Make no mistake. God is a generational God with a generational vision. From the time of Adam and Eve, His perspective of families was much greater than one family or one generation of families. God created us in His image and set us in a garden that looked like and felt like the kingdom of heaven for one reason, to expand His kingdom to heaven through a people He could call His children who would have His blood line and lineage. The earth was created to be a colony of heaven, a separate land mass by location, but a country under the authority and headship of heaven.

To bring it into a history lesson we have learned, America was originally a colony of Great Britain. This is why even today we can see characteristics of Great Britain in our culture and people. Earth, as a colony of the Kingdom of Heaven, was created to have the attributes, laws, and principles of heaven and the people would look like and act like those in heaven.

This is why we see God command Adam and Eve in Genesis 1:27-28, after He made them in His image, to go fill the earth and subdue it. This language is a reflection of God's mindset and perspective as a King, who like all Kings, desires to expand His kingdom. God created a family, one man and one women made in His image, who could expand the kingdom of heaven on earth through procreation; the DNA of the King and His Kingdom on earth perpetuating one generation after another.

Family was the establishment and paradigm God created on earth to make a family of sons and daughters who looked like and acted like the King, consequently creating a culture and society on earth that looked like and acted like the Kingdom of Heaven.

Battle of the Kingdoms

However, as we know, this was short-lived with the disobedience and sin of Adam and Eve. God, as a king, now had a problem. How was He going to expand His kingdom on this earth through a people who no longer acted like Him? They no longer carried His attributes, laws, or principles. Every King's goal and purpose is to expand their kingdom by defeating their foes and conquering their kingdoms. The foe of God became evident on that day in the garden; Satan and his kingdom of darkness.

In fact the very way God set up His plan of war against the Kingdom of Darkness was through a family. God said to Satan in the garden, "And I will put enmity between you and the woman, and between your seed and her Seed; He shall bruise your head, and you shall bruise His heel (Genesis 3:15)." God sent His only son, His family and lineage, through another family on earth (Mary and Joseph), to defeat Satan and His Kingdom.

"And from the days of John the Baptist until now the kingdom of heaven suffers violence, and the violent take it by force." Matthew 11:12

The battle of the Kingdoms is still raging today however in order to get as many souls for their kingdoms as possible. Satan was defeated at the cross through Christ, who made a way that we could be grafted back into the kingdom of heaven becoming sons and daughters of the king again. However Satan is not going down to Hell without stealing as many souls as he can. We must choose to serve the Kingdom of Heaven; victory is not automatic for us. According to John 10:10, one kingdom, that is the kingdom of darkness, has come to steal, kill, and destroy our families. The Kingdom of Heaven, Christ's kingdom, has come that we may have abundant life. This is the very reason why Jesus begins His model prayer to the disciples and to us by saying these words, "Our Father in heaven, Hallowed be Your name. Your kingdom come. Your will be done on earth as it is in heaven (Luke 11:2)." God still desires to expand His kingdom on earth today, He's just looking for a family who will choose to allow Him to do it through them.

Abraham's Choice

Today as I teach parents, one of my favorite passages of scriptures I like to teach from is Genesis 18:17-19. It really gives us a bird's eye view into God's heart for families and our calling as parents.

The scene as a conversation God has concerning Abraham right before He declares His judgment on Sodom and Gomorrah. The culture of which Abraham lived in was wicked, sexually perverse, self-centered and indulging. God's timing of judgement on this culture was about to be poured out, but before doing so, He wanted to make sure that He found the one family who He could use once again to assure His kingdom could continue to advance on this earth.

The passage goes like this, "And the LORD said, 'Shall I hide from Abraham what I am doing, since Abraham shall surely become a great and mighty nation, and all the nations of the earth shall be blessed in him? For I have known him, in order that he may command his children and his household after him, that they keep the way of the LORD, to do righteousness and justice, that the LORD may bring to Abraham what He has spoken to him' (Genesis 18:17-19)."

Abraham was not chosen by God to be the Father of the nations because He was a great anointed man who could do signs and wonders. No, Abraham was chosen by God because He was a Godly daddy who chose to use his seed, his family, to influence the earth with the principals and characteristics of the Kingdom of Heaven. God needed a family for such a time as that and He found one in Abraham.

I would like to pause and insert a prophetic word into the pages of this book for parents and families in this day and age we are living in as it pertains to this passage of scripture. I believe we are living in a time and season much like Abraham was living in. Our Sodom and Gomorrah is all around us with the transgender and homosexual agenda and the anti-Christ spirit that is growing greater and greater as the days goes. God's judgment is not far away.

> *God is speaking to those mothers and fathers who have an ear to hear what the spirit of the Lord is saying; this is our Abraham moment.*

God is seeking those who will answer the call to raise their children to do righteousness and justice in this Sodom and Gomorrah time and sea-son. He still desires to use families to fulfill His greatest call and purposes on this earth; to be His inheritance and to expand His kingdom on Earth. Abraham made the choice to battle on the side of the Kingdom of Heaven; his parenting was intentional and purpose-driven to the point he was willing to offer up his only son as a sacrifice to the Lord in an act of obedience. Are we ready to be that kind of parent who is willing to give our children completely and freely over to God for Him to do as He pleases? Are we ready to be a family for God's Kingdom who God can trust to influence and expand heaven on earth?

Pick-up, Aim, and Release

Chapter 2

Weapons of Warfare

There is a battle raging that is bigger than you or I, it is a battle of two kingdoms and the pawns in this enormous chest game is our families; the paradigm of which all inheritance and lineage of either the kingdom of darkness or the kingdom of heaven will pass down through. The greatest strategy of God's war, our war, against Satan and His kingdom of darkness is not in what we can do, the signs and wonders we can perform, or even how many people we can save, for if we do all that but lose our own children, sending the next generation into the hands of the Kingdom of Darkness, we will have failed to use our greatest weapon in this war and will have lost in our responsibility of the battle.

"Behold, children are a heritage from the LORD, The fruit of the womb is a reward. Like arrows in the hand of a warrior, So are the children of one's youth. Happy is the man who has his quiver full of them; They shall not be ashamed, But shall speak with their enemies in the gate."
Psalm 127:3-5

God ordained from the beginning of time that our children would become weapons of war; arrows in the hands of an army of parents who would know and understand how to use them in this great kingdom battle. I do not think many of us as parents today have come near to grasping the gravity and weight of the calling of ministry set before us as Christ following parents. I truly believe that as God creates life out of the seed of a husband and wife who love the Lord, He literally has handpicked those two parents to be called to the front lines. It is not all about sweet smelling babies, soccer games, family vacations, and school achievements. No, it is about a King and His vision for His kingdom played out in chosen vessels that will influence the earth to act like and be like heaven through their own family lineage. Having children, creating a family, is a generational and eternal calling to war, and it is the greatest honor and calling any one person will ever have. Family ministry is all about sharpening, preparing, and using the arrows of God, your children, to defeat the enemies' agenda in your family, in their generation, and in the generations to come.

Such a Time as This

It is really easy today, in such a time as this, to be full of fear and dread for what this culture and society holds for our families and children. It seems like every week on the news there is another terror attack, religious freedom being taken away, and victories seemingly on every side for the agenda of the kingdom of darkness to have its way with our young through homosexuality, transgender, and self-worship ideology. I often think to myself, what will it be like by the time my 6 year old becomes a teenager or young adult? Will she have gender bathrooms or locker rooms? Will she be able to carry a Bible to school or to the work place? Will she be able to worship Jesus in public or in her church?

The threat and the darkness is real, but as soon as I begin to feel troubled and worried, I remember God's word in Psalms. God predestined you and me to be parents for such a time as this and for our children to be born for such a time as this. Do not think the darkness of this world caught Him off guard in anyway.

He choose me and you because He needed a handful of parents who would be willing to receive His gift, the greatest gift on earth, but yet the greatest weapon on earth, for such a time as this. There has been no greater time in history to be parents and no greater opportunity in history to be warriors for the Kingdom of Heaven.

Defeating Our Enemy

Not only does that passage of scripture remind us as parents that the Lord has bestowed upon us the greatest gift and weapon in this war, but it promises us that if we honor and rise to the calling of parenting God's way, we will not be ashamed and our enemies will be defeated. You want to fight back against the homosexual agenda and against the anti-Christ spirit of this age, pour all your efforts into raising your children up in the fear of the Lord and as passionate active members of the body ready to do the work of Christ on this earth. What I can do as one person to expand God's kingdom is far less than what I can do if I raise up a Godly lineage and inheritance through the seed God has given me.

Pick-up

There is an element of trust and honor He has bestowed upon us; He has placed His greatest weapon of war in our hands and ultimately trusting that we are going to take up our weapon and do something with it. Far too many parents within the body of Christ today delegate their God-given responsibility to raise their children up in the Lord on the church.

Somehow, so many of us, even as God fearing moms and dads who are warriors in the army of God, don't even pick up our greatest spiritual weapon and calling.

We feel that if we love our children, feed them, give them shelter, teach them good morals, take them to church, give them things, and give them a good scholastic education, somehow we have done our job. It is amazing to me how little our responsibility of giving our children a spiritual education passes through the mind of moms and dads. They do not understand the treasure and weapon God has put before them and they never even pick up the calling. This to me is like being right in the middle of the war for your life and refusing to pick up the weapon handed to you to fight. A weapon is only powerful and helpful in a fight if you pick it up. God has called us to step into our calling as the number one spiritual leader and minister to our children; we can't afford not to do this. There is a generation we can look to in the Bible that did not pick up their God given calling and weapon and the results were devastating for those parents. Joshua 5 tells the story of God commanding Joshua to circumcise the children that came out of the wilderness. The reason told to us in Joshua 5:5-6 is "For all the people who came out [of Egypt] had been circumcised, but all the people born in the wilderness, on the way as they came out of Egypt, had not been circumcised. For the children of Israel walked forty years in the wilderness, till all the people who were men of war, who came out of Egypt, were consumed, because they did not obey the voice of the LORD."

The men of war, those who were meant to expand God's kingdom and battle His enemies, died in the dry dead wildness never seeing the promise land because they failed to do as God had asked them to do; they failed to disciple, sanctify, set apart, prepare, and give their children over to the ways of God. They failed to pick up their calling and do what God commanded them to do for the next generation. They neglected God's generational vision, and because of that, they died without ever seeing the promises of God fulfilled in their life. God found His vison and heart alive in Joshua to father the next generation.

God loves His children too much to watch them spiritually die in our hands; if we will not do it He will find someone else who will. This unfortunately is why the church has had to step up to being more than a help mate to parents; they have had to take on the calling of moms and dads because parents have neglected it. I don't know about you, but I want to see the promises of God in my family in my life time. I don't want anyone to take my place in the greatest calling of my life. Let's wake up, and pick up!

Aim

Here is our next challenge as warriors in this battle of the kingdoms for our families; we must not just pick up our calling and shape the greatest weapons God has set before us, our children, but we must decide to aim our weapon at its target. Let's be honest, anyone can pick up a gun, but without proper aim it really is not going to help many in battle.

A weapon is intended to be picked up and then aimed at its receiving target… Spiritually, where do you want to see your children go, what do you want to see them do?

We must begin to spend time with the Lord and ask Him what His calling and purposes are for our children and begin to aim them in that direction. Family ministry is all about the shaping, disciplining, and preparing of our children for God's will and purposes for their life. There are some callings and purposes we all share as children of God, and there are some that are specific to each individual's giftings.

I believe if God has given us this great and mighty weapon, He is able to teach us where to aim it. Go before Him, get a clear vision, and then press into that vision.

I want to share a very personal experience that happened in our family that relates to this mandate. When our first child was born, I was not walking with the Lord. I had been backslidden for eight years and married my high school sweetheart that was not saved. So when we had our son, Tristan, there was absolutely no stirring concerning parenting being a calling of Lord. However, it only took two years and two miscarriages after Tristan, before the Holy Spirit began to woo me back again. Soon, through trials and tribulations, my husband was saved and we were walking with the Lord. We had begun to work in ministry through a church plant when the Holy Spirit began to deal with us specifically about Tristan's calling. It was a night of revival and Tristan, age 7 at the time, was up at the altar during ministry time in the middle of it all. One of my friends was watching Tristan do this and came over to me and spoke a prophetic word into my ear. She spoke to me that Tristan has the spirit of Samuel on him and would become both a priest and prophet unto the Lord. I immediately felt my spirit leap for joy. What she did not know was that Tristan's middle name was Samuel.

As I spent the next two weeks keeping this word very close to my heart, the Lord began to speak to me.

He told me that Tristan was the name we had chosen, but Samuel was the name He had chosen.

He spoke into my spirit that we needed to begin to call Tristan by His God given name Samuel. Now my husband was still a baby Christian and I wasn't sure how he would react to doing something like that. So I asked the Lord to speak to Him before I did so, that His heart would already be prepared for what I was going to say. Two weeks went by before I felt the release to mention this to my husband. As I said the words, "There is something I need to speak to you concerning Tristan", he finished my sentence by saying "God already told me you want to change his name to Samuel." Well that was the only confirmation we both needed. The next day we talked to Tristan about it and he couldn't have been more excited.

In fact, here is the amazing thing. Tristan ended up getting water baptized on his eighth birthday, going down as Tristan coming up as Samuel. A year later we went to court and had his legal named changed to Samuel.

I believe God Choose Samuel's eighth birthday because it is the number of new beginnings. He was speaking to not just Samuel that day, but to us as his parents that it was time for a new beginning. We must start to pick up our calling and aim our weapon. Every time I called his name I was reminded of the calling on his life. We have prayed into, declared it, and discipled him towards it. Well, Samuel is now a senior in High School and has led an after school Bible study since the seventh grade, preached many times in youth, and will be pursuing ministry at college next year. I believe had we not heard the voice of God and was obedient to do as He said, the blessings on our family would not be what they are today.

Release

Here is the last thing I want to discuss in this chapter. Again, when we think about using a weapon, particularly a bow and arrow, three things come to mind; pick it up, aim, and release.

> *If we pick up are weapons, our children, and we aim them at their God given target, but never release them to do it, nothing but frustration and failure will ever be produced from our efforts.*

There is nothing more frustrating to someone than to be trained in a certain area, given a gift and ability to do something, only to never be able to do it. It's kind of like teaching a child how to ride a bike, but never allowing them to ride.

> *Family ministry is not just about preparing our children for their calling; it is about releasing them to do it.*

We must trust that what God has called them to do and what He has equipped them to do through us, they are able to do it. We must learn to release them into ministry… at the age they are now, not just when they leave our homes.

Again we are going to look at scripture to give us a better understanding of this. This is probably my second to third favorite subject to teach on. I am going to take you right to the family above all families in the Bible; Jesus and His heavenly father and earthy mother. I want to start by pointing out the release Jesus received from His father on the day of His water baptism. Jesus had been discipled and prepared. His mother had taken up her weapon and calling and knew very much what her son was called to do; God had made sure of that. God Himself had aimed His son and poured into Him, filling Him with the Holy Spirit. Now, it was time for a release. As the dove, the Holy Spirit, came upon Jesus that day in the baptismal waters anointing Him for ministry, Jesus' father said, "This is My beloved Son, in whom I am well pleased (Matthew 3:17)." These few words of affirmation released Jesus to do what He had been trained for… battle.

Our children are longing for us to affirm them into ministry. They need to know we believe in them and are pleased with who they are in Christ. This kind of affirmation gives them the confidence to "do the stuff".

But this is not where it ended with Jesus. As in the order God established for a father and a mother to raise their children up in the Lord, Mary had her own moment of release. Many of us know the story well; Jesus's first miracle of turning the water into wine. Sometimes we brush by the significance of Mary's part in this story of Jesus' first miracle and the start of His earthly ministry. It was noticed at the wedding that the wine had run out. Mary looked at her son and told Him the news. Jesus then replied to her, "Woman, what does your concern have to do with Me? My hour has not yet come (John 2:4)." He knew exactly what Mary was saying between the lines and all it took was one simple statement of release for Jesus to step into His calling. Mary said to the servants, "Whatever He says to you, do it (John 2:5)." Jesus needed to hear from His mother that she believed in Him and had confidence He could do what He was called to do.

There is no age to the spirit so as they grow and learn, give them a safe place within your home ministry to do that which they are called to do in the Lord. Let them know that they are weapons of God made for battle and then release them to do battle for Jesus!

Biblical Blueprint

Chapter 3

Aaron and His Sons

"And you shall bring his sons and clothe them with tunics. You shall anoint them, as you anointed their father, that they may minister to Me as priests; for their anointing shall surely be an everlasting priesthood throughout their generations." Exodus 40:14-15

God established Family Ministry through the priesthood of Aaron. Moses was not only instructed to bring Aaron to be anointed as a Holy Priest unto the Lord, but He was also instructed to bring Aaron's sons. The priesthood was established to be a family ministry; one generation to another creating a perpetual lifestyle of worship before God. With this order established, God set in motion the blueprint for family ministry.

New Testament Priesthood

Many may argue that the ways of the Old Testament do not apply to us today as New Testament believers, but the scriptures tell us in Colossians 2:17 and Hebrews 8:5 that the tabernacle and the laws of which to worship within, was a copy and shadow of the original in heaven. Although Jesus fulfilled the law and the acts of worship in the Old Testament making them not necessary today, the principles and foreshadowing still apply to us as New Testament believers. In fact, Jesus makes it clear in 1 Peter 2:5 that we are to continue the role of the priesthood "You also, as living stones, are being built up a spiritual house, a holy priesthood, to offer up spiritual sacrifices acceptable to God through Jesus Christ."

Generational Vision

God's thoughts and motives reached far beyond one man named Aaron. They reached into the depths of eternity and established the ancient paths of His Holy priesthood, those who would serve and worship Him all the days of their lives. When we accept the commission of 1 Peter 2:5, to become Holy Priest unto the Lord, we must also accept the commission of family ministry. What God has established he will never unestablish... His word and ways are the same yesterday, today, and forever. We must get beyond the "me", and get to the "we", and take our children, that being your own children or the ones the Lord has given to us in the next generation to mentor and disciple, by the hand and teach them how to worship and serve the Lord.

God knew that in order to keep a Holy line of priest, the family must worship and serve Him together. Their life would have to become a life of worship, their home centered on serving the Lord. The children would grow up worshipping with their father and mother, learning each day what it meant to worship God, why they must worship God, and how they must worship God. They would be drenched in the presence of the Lord as it filled their home and their lives on a daily basis. For a priest and their family, serving God was not something they did, it was who they were. The household of a priest was established to live their lives serving and worshipping God.

"And these words which I command you today shall be in your heart. You shall teach them diligently to your children, and shall talk of them when you sit in your house, when you walk by the way, when you lie down, and when you rise up. You shall bind them as a sign on your hand, and they shall be as frontlets between your eyes. You shall write them on the doorposts of your house and on your gates." Deuteronomy 6:6-9

Stepping into Our Role

The truth is, families of God have struggled to stay afloat as the pressure of socialization and higher education has drowned out the importance of a spiritual education in our homes. We go our separate ways at home and we even go our separate ways at church, never fulfilling our mandate of family ministry as priests unto the Lord. George Barna statistics tells us that 75% of all children by the time they are 18 leave the church never to return again. We have forgotten the ancient paths. We have forgotten how to pass down our Godly inheritance. How much of a priority have we made family ministry in our homes? Are we stepping into the call of the priesthood and created a perpetual generation of worshipers? How many parents can honestly say they pray with their children in their homes on a daily basis? Do we read the bible together in our homes, or is this time just set aside for church? George Barna statistics tell us that only 1 out of 10 families in the body of Christ will ever read the Bible together or pray in a given week. Do we truly have a house that serves God? Could it be we have neglected to make our priesthood a family ministry?

I am convinced that one of the keys to having a Godly family and keeping our Godly heritage in our homes, through our children and through our children's' children, is in the call to make the Holy Priesthood a family ministry once again. We must worship God in our homes and with our children.

37

Our priesthood is through the blood of Jesus, and His blood must wash off our garments unto our children's garments.

The Ancient Paths

I am convinced there is no other way to keep a family from becoming broken and in disarray in this time in history but to engage in and purposefully pursue family ministry. There are too many battles raging; too many temptations pulling our families apart. While the evil one has sought to destroy the very foundation of families from the very beginning of time starting with Adam and Eve, the only thing that can guarantee the protection of our homes, our families, and our children, is our mandate to serve and worship God together.

God said in Jeremiah 18:15, that Israel was scattered and broken because she had forgotten the ancient paths, let it not be said of us that we have forgotten the ancient paths of old; the ways established for us through the Holy Priesthood. In Exodus 29, God paints a beautiful picture of each one of our calls to family ministry in the priesthood. From the garments of the priest, to the washing of their hands, to the laying of hands on the sacrifice, to the blood that anointed their ear, thumb, feet, and garments, to the wave offerings, to the heave offerings, to the eating of the sacrifice; father to son did it all together. The father's heart was turned to his son, and his son's heart was turned to his father. They were, together, consecrated, set apart, and holy before the Lord; truly a house that served the Lord.

Today our call is to return to the ancient paths of the stones laid out before us in God's Holy word. As each one of us is called to be a Holy Priest unto the Lord, we are also called to take our children by the hand and do the work of family ministry through that priesthood.

Today, the priesthood is not only father and sons; it is mothers and daughters, fathers and daughters, and Mothers and sons. The Holy Spirit calls each one of us under the blood of Jesus; He is no respecter of persons. As we are anointed, they are anointed. As we are covered in the blood, let them be covered in the blood. As we serve the Holy one, they must serve the Holy one. As we sacrifice, let them sacrifice. As we offer our lives up, they must offer up their lives. Teach them to serve; teach them to worship. We must get back to the ancient paths.

Religion versus Relationship

Chapter 4

Religion versus Relationship

Profane Fire

> *"Then Nadab and Abihu, the sons of Aaron, each took his censer and put fire in it, put incense on it, and offered profane fire before the LORD, which He had not commanded them." Leviticus 10:1*

As we establish the blueprint of priesthood from the Old Testament to the New, let us be careful not to receive it into our hearts to be rooted in generational religion and not relationship. This was the mistake of Nadab and Abihu, two of Aaron's sons.

I would be amiss to use Aaron and His sons as an example of family ministry done right without pointing out the example in this passage of family ministry done wrong. In Leviticus 10, a short but powerful story unfolds, that if we let it, becomes a revelation for us and a pinned instruction on what to do and not to do in family ministry. Aaron's sons, Nadab and Abihu, decided on their own to burn incense unto the Lord as an offering. The scriptures tell us however in Leviticus 10:1 that this was a profaned fire before the Lord. Why? Didn't it seem right for them to do what they had learned from their dad all of those years? Within that same scripture the answer is given to us by God, "He [God] had not commanded them." God goes on to say to Moses and Aaron in Leviticus 10: 3, "By those who come near

Me I must be regarded as holy and before all the people I must be glorified."

Hearing and Obeying the Voice of God

The question must be raised that if Nadab and Abihu did not receive the command from God to offer up a burnt offering, could they not hear the voice of God? Could it be that Aaron in all of His modeling before His sons, instructing them on how to perform a burnt offering, a heave offering, and do the acts of worship required by the law of God, forgot to teach them how to hear and yield to the voice of God?

We must be careful that we do not make the same mistake Aaron did and teach our children how to do the acts of worship to God without the relationship with God.

I fear too many kids are being raised up in church, holding on to their parent's coat tails, going through the motions of Christianity but never grounded in a relationship with Christ themselves. And when the world has a chance to influence them, they cannot rightfully discern His voice in their ears verses the worlds.

We do not want to take them by the hand and show them our religion, but take them by the hand and introduce them to a relationship with Christ. You can only hear God's voice when you are close enough to Him to hear His whisper in your ear. We must first teach them how to walk in a relationship with Christ, seek His voice for themselves, and how to obey that voice. If we do not, we have only taught them how to perform in a religious ceremony, not how to engage in a relationship with God and authentic worship. It is not enough to just say, "Do as I do; read your word, pray before you eat and go to bed, go to church..." This will not yield a perpetual generation of worshippers, but instead a perpetual generation of religious people. We must teach our children to seek out a relationship with God for themselves; to seek His presence, His voice and leading, and to offer up an offering out of their heart, not out of tradition and religion.

Knowing Who God is

"By those who come near Me I must be regarded as holy and before all the people I must be glorified." Leviticus 10:3

In order to hear God's voice and walk in His ways we must know who God is. God is Holy and His holiness requires honor and glory. There is a tremendous deficit of honor and reverence for God's holiness today in our churches and our homes. We have taught one generation after another how to "play" church, living one way in the church house and living another way at home. We put up a facade for the world to see that brings **us** glory, all while we walk in disobedience and ignorance of God's way and will.

I believe that day when Aaron's sons offered up a profane and defiled offering, it was not just because they could not discern God's voice and did something God did not ask them to do. This was simply a result of not having a relationship with God, and in not having a relationship with God, they did not know God and His ways.

The incredible deficit of fear and reverence to God in our churches and homes today is not due to intentional disobedience, but due to a lack of authentic relationship with God and wisdom and knowledge of who He is and His ways.

God's Fire Versus Man's

As a result of Aaron's son's profane fire, God sent His own fire to consume them (Leviticus 10:2). When we allow our family, our children, to "play" church out of religion verses relationship, the profane offering to God will result in the death of their spirits and eventually, the eternal damnation of their souls.

The greatest tragedy is to go through our lives thinking as parents that we have taught our children how to worship the Lord, and in the end we find that the aroma that went up to the Lord was a stitch of religion from man's fire verses a sweet aroma from God's.

When our family worship is out of relationship with God, the fire we produce is the fire of God. But when we worship out of tradition or religious mandates, the fire we will produce will be fleshly and defiled. We might for a time be satisfied within the confines of manmade fire, but in the end we will become empty, dead in our spirits, and have raised the next generation to do the same with the same results.

This is why we focus on family ministry that is led by the spirit and not out of tradition and religion.

I believe that one generation after another has been cursed with the spirit of Nadab and Abihu's profane worship because we have not taught our children how to have a relationship with God; to know His ways and will and hear His voice for themselves. In the chapters that lie ahead we are going on a step by step journey into how to lead your family in to ministry lead by the spirit of God, establishing relationship verses religion. The spirit of God is His presence, His character and nature, and is His voice. Without Him, the Holy Spirit, being the center of our family ministry, it will be impossible to raise up a generation of authentic worshippers to Christ.

The Domino Effect
of Satan's Lie

Chapter 5

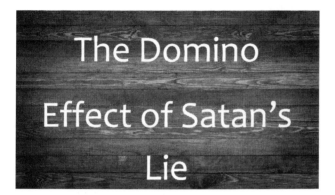

The Lie Satan has Fed Us

Several years ago, I was addressing a Children's Pastor at a church I had a relationship with. She was (obviously) frustrated and sent out an email to all parents forcing them to volunteer time in Children's church for a series of revival services that was going on out of normal service times. I understood her frustration of not getting enough volunteers and that she wanted to be able to enjoy the services herself as well. So I suggested to her that she not make available children's church at all and use this as an opportunity for the families to worship and experience God together. The answer, although in so many ways true and extremely common in the church today, was heartbreaking to me and to our heavenly Father.

She said to me that kids today do not feel comfortable worshipping with their parents, and parents and leaders do not want to have to deal with misbehaving kids in service. The fact is, she was right. If you were to ask a room full of kids from ages 8 or 9 to 13 if they feel totally comfortable engaging in spirit-filled worship and encountering the presence of God in front of their parents, the majority, hands down, would say no. I know, I have asked the question many times. And to be honest, the majority, not all, but majority of parents feel either the same way or at the very least do not want their kids in the service because of being distracted by them or having to deal with their misbehavior.

These mindsets in families have been established unfortunately because of the lie the church has bought into from Satan. However, just because something is the reality of the state of the church and her families today does not make it biblical or right in the eyes of God.

> *If any one group should feel comfortable worshipping and engaging in the presence of God together, it should be families.*

Satan's devastating lie to the church has to do with how we see children today in the body. So much of the body still sees children as not part of the church, incapable of encountering and responding to the presence of God. They see them as simply children who need to be babysat or at best told the stories of Jesus in order to get saved... that is it.

The Domino Effect

The lie of Satan has a domino effect on the whole body, especially the kids and families.

> *Satan's purpose and goal in propagating this lie is to alienate the children of God from having a deep spiritual relationship with Jesus, from feeling like they have an influence in the Kingdom, and to separate families physically, emotionally, and spiritually.*

As we have discussed earlier, Satan's agenda is always to steal, kill, and destroy the next generation one child at a time.

When the church begins to buy into the lie of Satan concerning children, it grossly effects how the body can function with children and families. There is nothing wrong with separating ministries by age if it is done right and there is a balance of family ministry. I personally am a state director for an international children's ministry.

However, when decades ago we began to separate families within the worship services of our church (parents going one way children going the other) that is when the lie of Satan began to take root, causing the first domino to fall on the new found children's leaders and pastors of the church. They took on the mindset that there was a reason children should be separated and not take part in the "adult" functions of worship, word, and ministry in the church. They began to approach how they minister to children differently.

Children were given a watered down, dumbed down version of Christianity that left no room for genuine deep relationship with Jesus, hearing His voice, feeling His presence, or ministering under His power and anointing.

Children in most churches today are not taught how to engage in genuine worship to the Lord. All too often we make children's church worship entertainment and mimic sessions full of praise and dance moves, dismissing any opportunity for them to actually commune with Jesus through the Holy Spirit. So now we have head Pastors and leaders who have bought into the lie taking the first move to separate families and alienate children from encountering Jesus in a real way.

The second domino to fall is on the parents. Up until that point the families that were devoted to God spent time in worship at home together and at church. But when the church, the pastors and leaders that parents trusted, began to separate their kids from the "adult" services and from themselves, a silent suggestion that became an unbiblical truth within many parents started to grow; kids cannot engage in worship and ministry to the Lord alongside me or other adults. This lie began to influence how parents looked at family worship at home. Coupled with the business of the hour in which we live in, it became easy just to allocate their responsibility to the children leaders in the church. If family ministry exist today, all too often it is centered on surface Christianity with meal time and bedtime prayer. There are no real encounters of God's presence together as a family. Presence-driven family worship is almost obsolete in the church or at home. The last domino falls into the lap of our children themselves. When from the head of the church, down through the head ministries, down to the parents themselves treat children as second class citizens in the kingdom, not worth being taken seriously, or given a place to pursue the presence of God and minister as part of the body, children themselves begin to believe the lie.

We have, by our actions, told children that they do not have the same spirit living in them as we do, and they cannot possibly function as part of the body until they reach some magical age of older teen to young adult.

Tradition and religion have perpetuated an unbiblical perspective of children that makes it impossible for us to see them as spirit beings, who long to encounter their heavenly Father through worship just the same as us. Yet Jesus said in Mark 10:14-15, "Let the little children come to Me, and do not forbid them; for of such is the kingdom of God. Assuredly, I say to you, whoever does not receive the kingdom of God as a little child will by no means enter it." Jesus did not say "tell them about me", no, He commanded us to allow the Children to come to Him; to encounter Him, feel Him, touch Him, and hear Him. If Jesus desired this and pointed to a child as to how we are all supposed to enter into the Kingdom, don't you think we should believe they can?

When a child comes into the church and is never given opportunity to encounter Jesus in a genuine worship experience and to minister as part of the body, they begin themselves to believe they can't. Again, they have no release or affirmation to counter that. This cultivates the ground for the lie of Satan to take root in them making them uncomfortable to even try to engage in worship as we do, much less alongside of us. If there is no real family worship going on at home to teach and cultivate your kids, when they get into an environment that requires them to worship as a family, they shut down, don't know what to do, and feel uncomfortable, resulting often in misbehavior.

Sunday Family Services are not Working

In the recent years some churches have felt a nudging from the Holy Spirit, or at least a desire to respond to the echoing need for family worship, by creating a family worship Sunday. Many use the fifth Sunday as a way to create an opportunity for family worship days. Although the attempt is heartfelt, these Sundays are not genuine family worship experiences. They are at best an adult worship service where the kids are invited in. Most cases, if you were to look around the sanctuary while these services are going on, you will see kids on their electronic devices, coloring, or misbehaving out of sheer boredom. This is not families who are in unity by the spirit going after the presence of God together. If these services do anything it just frustrates the parents, and allows Satan to use it to confirm to parents his lie that their kids can't handle spiritual things.

I believe that this option is the last step to regenerating family worship, but the first step has to start in the home; re-training a generation of families how to pursue God's presence and His ways as a lifestyle.

We must renew our minds as parents to see our children as spirit beings that can and desire to pursue God just like us. Secondly, we must retrain the church to see children with a new mindset that is biblical and kingdom minded.

Then, and only then, can we fully see the families of God walk in unity and as God intended as families of priests who serve and worship God day and night.

Second Half

Creative and practice tools to presence-driven Family worship

Biblical Worship

Chapter 6

Misunderstood Doctrine

Now that we have established God's generational vision for families, a biblical blueprint for family ministry through the priesthood, and why this is not happening in our churches and homes, we must now re-group and establish practical steps to getting back to the ancient ways and paths of God. If worship is the roadway and call for the families of God to do together, we must define what true authentic and biblical worship is so that our family will not be like Aaron's sons and offer up a profane and religious offering to God.

Worship is one of the fundamental doctrines of the church, yet it seems to be one of the most misunderstood doctrines within the body today. It is important we first establish a biblical definition of what worship is so that we will have our right footing and foundation to stand on when leading our family in Presence- driven worship in our home.

Perhaps the one sure thing I know about worship is that it has become a sensitive subject within the body of Christ, and in some cases has been a divisive subject that has torn many places of worship in two. After seeing these worship wars played out many times throughout the years, I have begun to realize that at the root of this war for each individual involved is an unbiblical and skewed definition and foundation of what true authentic worship really is, why God ordained it, and what its true purpose is in us as believers.

If you were to ask a room full of children who consistently attend church what worship is, the answer you would get would sound a bit like this: "Worship is when we sing songs in church". On the surface, that seems like a logical and true answer, but is that really worship?

The answer the next generation of believers has given to define worship should be an indicator to us of what we have made worship to be and how we have modeled it before them.

Authentic Biblical Worship

Today worship is widely defined by the two fast songs and one slow song we sing in our adult and children congregations. It has become a place we go, not a lifestyle we live. However, this is not a biblical definition of what true worship is all about. Worship in its simplest definition is one's heart, body, soul, and spirit given over to God for Him to do as He pleases. Worship is not to be defined by the songs we sing or the music we play, or even the place we go, but instead a life lived in obedience and sacrifice through Christ, honoring Him as the giver of life and Lord of all. All the rest of what we call worship is simply manifestations or acts of the true worship within our heart.

The reality is worship has become a portion of a church program rather than a required way of living in order to become a holy dwelling place of the living God. Worship was never intended to be a song, but ones heart posture to the Lord lived out in a lifestlye of devotion.

Mary Magdalene's Worship

Mary Magdalene extravagantly worshiped Jesus without ever singing a tune and without ever playing an instrument. Her worship so moved Jesus that she was the only one He ever mentioned that would be talked about wherever the gospel was preached. Isn't that amazing?

We have so defined in our culture of church and Christianity today worship by the song we sing and the instruments we play that we have truly lost sight of what authentic worship is. As a result we now have perpetual generations who are being raised up to give perverted worship to God much like Aaron's sons did.

In Isaiah 1:11 God says, "To what purpose is the multitude of your sacrifices to Me?" Says the LORD. "I have had enough of burnt offerings of rams and the fat of fed cattle. I do not delight in the blood of bulls, or of lambs or goats." God was saying to them that their sacrifices of animals had no real power or purpose. In fact they were so powerless that they had to continue to do sacrifice one animal after another to make up for all their sins, and it still was not good enough. If you read that whole chapter you will see the continual sacrifice became so routine that it just became religious and did not move the heart of God whatsoever. They, in most cases, even mixed their worship to God with idol worship to the point that idols shared the same space within God's holy temple. They would perform their worship rituals and then go out and do evil. They had a heart issue and God was really tired and disgusted with the whole thing.

I believe in many ways we have allowed our worship in church culture today to become much like theirs in the Old Testament. God, I believe, is disgusted with what we have made worship to be. It has become so predictable, so ritualized, so robotic and fleshly, that it has affected our very relationship with God the Father.

Frankly many churches today, both in adult service and kids services, I think God looks down and says, "I do not delight in substitution for the real thing. Your bull and calf worship has no power to move me".

Have you ever wondered why Jesus said to the woman at the well, "But the hour is coming, and now is, when the true worshipers will worship the Father in spirit and truth; for the Father is seeking such to worship Him (John 4:23)?" Jesus didn't say that the Father was seeking out those who could heal the sick, those who could prophecy, and those who could preach or teach, although those things are pleasing to the Lord and manifestations of our worship. But Jesus said that the Father was seeking worshipers, but not just any worshipers, but those who will worship in spirit and in truth. This was the heart of Mary Magdalene; worship in spirit and in truth.

The heart of the Father in heaven cries out to tabernacle and dwell with His children, and worship in truth defined by God's word, and worship in Spirit defined by who God is, is the only way He can be with His children; that is me and you. God is beckoning a generation that will leave the comfortable place of tradition, religion, and complacency, and surrender all of themselves to a lifestyle of extravagant worship not defined by man but defined by God.

Why is Worship so Important?

> *Worship was the very road God established to lead us into communion, fellowship, and presence of our heavenly Father.*

Worship is the roadway we MUST TAKE to grow as a believer. Our very relationship to God and Jesus; the level in which we grow in the Lord, hear His voice, feel His presence, do His will on this earth is defined by worship. Worship is the path that God has given us to stepping into the spirit where He is. If you want to go see a friend that does not live in your neighborhood, you must get in the car and follow the road to their house. Likewise, if we want to see Jesus, experience His presence, talk to Him, and hear His voice, we must enter into worship. That is the road we must take; there is no other way.

God is spirit and we must worship Him in Spirit; worship gives us access to the spirit realm.

I believe our culture of perverted counterfeit worship in the church today has distanced the children of God from him. We can't hear his voice, we do not experience His manifested presence, and we lack the ability to see the reality of God and the spirit realm because our worship has no power to move us into the spirit and to move the heart of God.

What Worship Does in Us

A Chameleon Lizard has the ability to change colors in order to look like whatever environment it is touching. If it is near a leaf, it becomes bright green. If it is on a branch, it becomes brown. Did you know we have the ability to do that same thing? This is why the Lord requires that we not be unequally yoked with whom we are in close relationship with. Who or what we are around and touch has the ability to change the character and nature of who we are. It is no different when it comes to our spiritual walk.

You are made up of three parts, just like God has three parts. You have a flesh which is what we see on the outside. You have a soul which is what you feel and think. And you have a spirit which at the point of salvation is filled with the Holy Spirit who lives and dwells within you. The more we worship, the more we connect with the person of the Holy Spirit within us. The more we connect with the person of the Holy Spirit within us, the more we touch God and His kingdom. As the environment of God's presence (His Kingdom) begins to touch us again and again through worship, liken to a chameleon lizard, we begin to change physically in our flesh. But not only that, we change in our soul and spirit as well.

The change in our body, soul, and spirit, although it can be, is usually not quick and instantaneous. It's like a cup of water and red food coloring. If I put one red drop of food coloring in a glass, what color will the water turn? Not quite red but an orangey color, right? But what if I add many drops of red food coloring? The water will turn completely red. Just like this water and food coloring, the more we touch heaven and are surrounded by the presence of God, the more we change into the character of Christ and of heaven. Every time we express our worship, our love, obedience, and reverence to God, the more God's presence comes down and dwells with us and changes us

(James 4:8). But as it says in 2 Corinthians 3:18, the change is from glory to glory; one drop at a time.

This is why worship is so important to God. When you were dead in your sins giving your heart over to Satan and worldly things you were being changed to look like the world. But as you begin to worship God you begin to receive the residue of Heaven instead.

Who's in the Driver's Seat of Your Family?

Worship looks a little like this: you're setting in a car you call your life, and in the driver seat is whatever you choose to worship; that is to love above everything else, honor above everything else, and obey above everything else.

The object or deity that you worship could be Jesus, or money, or anything you are devoted to. No matter what it is, it will be the one thing that determines where you go and what you do in this journey called life.

When you worship something or someone, they hold your outermost love, respect, and devotion; meaning they hold the power to your life. Worship is an issue of the heart. Whatever or whomever you decide to worship, no question, will have your heart. We all worship something; it is just a matter of what.

This is why family worship is so incredibly important. As parents, we decide who is in that driver seat of our family by whom we worship and who or what we place in power of our family's life. There is no doubt that in the world, and even in the church, many parents have placed money, success, things, and the lust of the world through demonic strongholds in the driver seat of their family. Who or what is driving your family?

The Role Music Plays

Singing and playing songs of worship, although not to be defined as worship itself, can be a manifestation or act of our worship. In fact it is the very first act of worship that we see ever being expressed to God in heaven before earth was ever created (Revelations 4:8-11 John describes the scene of heaven). This act of worship is a natural reaction out of a heart felt love and devotion the angels and creatures of heaven have for God as their creator. If you noticed, their act of worship does not stop, their love and devotion to God drives them into a lifestyle of worship day and night. Through the fabric of the Bible, music, hymns, and psalms were used to express one's heart to God. God Himself commands us to use music in our worship. Here is just one of the many scriptures: "Sing to the Lord a new song (Psalms 149:1)."

The greatest worship songs ever created were first birthed in one's heart as they were reaching up to heaven to encounter God, and God was reaching down to encounter them.

It is said that music is the language of the world; no matter where you live and what language you speak, music speaks to the heart of humanity. Study after study shows that unconsciously as we sing a song those words are memorized and placed into our soul to become truth to us. Music has powerful consequences. This truth does not pass by Satan, who theologians believe might have been the high angel in charge of worship in heaven. Satan has led the charge in perverting music and songs to speak his lies into humanity's heart. This is why it is so incredibly important that you monitor what type of music your family listens to and sing along with.

If we use songs as a way to manifest and come into agreement with what our own heart feels and knows about Christ, then they become an act of worship. But if we are simply regurgitating a song because it is what we are supposed to do in a "worship" service, the only thing it will do is deceive us into thinking we have worshiped when all we have done is sent up a stitch of hypocrisy to the Lord. In the presence-filled worship experiences I am going to suggest to you, music, in most cases, is simply used to keep our focus on the Lord, and to set the atmosphere for the presence of God.

Presence-Driven Family Worship

Chapter 7

What is Presence-Driven Family Worship?

Now that we have defined biblical worship, why worship is so important, and what it does to us as we worship, let's dive right into exploring presence-driven family worship.

Authentic presence-driven family worship is an intentional pursuit of God's presence from both adults and kids within a family.

It is a worship experience of which all ages are encountering the presence of Jesus on some level and where each family member walks away been changed body, soul, and spirit. It is not worship engaging just the kids or just the adults, but everyone.

Why is Presence-Driven Worship so Important?

We have already talked about what happens to our body, soul, and spirit as we worship authentically. Now let's focus on carrying those same principles into family worship. There is no question the family of the modern age is under attack. Families within the body are ripped apart with divorce rates equal to that of the world. Children are growing up broken, rejected, and confused as to what a family is supposed to even look like under the prevailing winds of the homosexual agenda. There is a spirit of rebellion and resentment that has saturated many homes. The truth is, even in the best Jesus-following families, we have issues and attacks on all sides. I believe even more so because we are following Christ and threatening the kingdom of darkness.

A lifetime of the greatest pastoral and Christian counseling cannot do for our families what one moment together in the presence of God can do.

The Holy Spirit is our great counselor, comforter, healer, and truth giver. He is the person of Christ on earth. When we create opportunity for Him to have His way in family worship suddenly what was in disunity comes into unity; what was broken is healed.

There is no greater intimate moment in our family than when we engage in presence-driven worship together. This is why there is such a focus on worship in our corporate services; it brings unity and oneness in the spirit of believers, which in turn brings a greater measure of the outpouring and presence of Jesus. We see this biblical model played out in the followers of Jesus who were found praying and worshipping in the upper room, and in one accord the scripture says (Acts 2:1). On that day the baptism of the Holy Spirit poured out for all believers.

When we engage in presence-driven worship with our families, it brings us into such a place of vulnerability and intimacy with God and with each other.

As we open our hearts wide to encounter the spirit of God and to allow Him to have His way in us, we likewise open our hearts wide before each other allowing each person to see the others real heart and self.

Suddenly we see each other through the Spirit of God and all the pre-conceived notions, fleshly agendas, walls of protection and defense, and skewed thoughts of each other, is over powered by the love of God and His truth that is in the room. We are not operating in the flesh, but by the spirit. This is incredibly powerful for families who live together and know and experience the greatest and ugliest of moments with each other.

Worshipping in a place of intimacy and vulnerability keeps us focused on seeing each other through God's heart and not our own, cultivating love and forgiveness towards each other. We, one drop at a time, take on the mind, will, and emotions of Christ for each other.

There is no greater experience families can have together; no vacation, no sports game, no board game, nothing compares to presence-driven family worship.

Introduction to the Tabernacle Model

Chapter 8

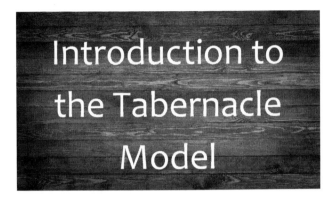

Object Lessons

So this is where the rubber meets the road in presence-driven family worship. You are about to move from learning about it, to doing it. As I give you a practical step-by- step blueprint to activating your family in presence driven worship, I want to draw your attention to the importance of object lessons.

When drawing kids into any kind of spiritual encounter with the Lord the greatest tool you can use is object lessons.

In fact, I don't hesitate to say that this goes for you and me as adults as well. The Bible is full of taking the things in the natural to bring people into the supernatural. The most common object lesson in the Bible that is still used today is communion. The bread and wine/juice is a very natural way to worship Jesus in the supernatural or in the spirit. If we allow it, communion can become a tool to having a presence-driven worship experience.

The Tabernacle of Moses

Communion is just one example; the ways are as endless and creative as the Holy Spirit. In trying to lead families into the place of a presence-driven family worship experience I have learned that God already has a step by step outline in his word, and if we just follow it, it leads us right back to Him every time.

> *The Tabernacle of Moses was constructed for God to have a way to tabernacle or dwell among His children.*

Although Jesus came, died for our sins, rose on the third day, and sent the Holy Spirit, His spirit, to dwell with man, the foreshadowing and reflection brings revelation and tangibility to our worship. In fact, 1 Corinthians 6:19 makes it clear that we are the New Testament temple or tabernacle, "Or do you not know that your body is the temple of the Holy Spirit who is in you, whom you have from God, and you are not your own?" Nothing God established in the Old Testament is ever destroyed or un-established in the New; it only becomes a foreshadowing or reflection of things to come. Let me give you one simple reflection you might find interesting. There are 6 furniture pieces or places of worship in the Tabernacle. The number six in the Bible is always a reflection of humanity, pointing the Tabernacle right back to us.

> *Every place of worship and furniture piece of the Tabernacle of old has significance to us in our pursuit for God's presence; it is the natural brought to the supernatural.*

The Shadow of the Outer Court

The tabernacle of Moses consisted of three major areas; the outer court, the inner court or sanctuary, and inner most court or the most holy. God also has three parts to Him; Father, Son, and Holy Spirit. So, we can begin to see that the tabernacle was actually a shadow of God Himself, each section representing a part of the trinity of God. But as we just discussed the Tabernacle was also a reflection of you and me. Do we have three parts to us? Yes, Body, soul, and Spirit.

The outer court was sectioned off by a cloth fence. This area was completely uncovered and was lit by the natural light of the sun. This was the foreshadowing of God's son (sun) that was to be the light of the world according to John 8:12. Often, Jesus referred to us as sheep and He as the shepherd. If you look at the outer court, it could be recognized as a fenced in pasture for sheep. There was a gate or a door on the east side of the court and in John 10:9 Jesus is referred to as the door where we find pasture.

Some people try to get close to God by climbing or jumping over the door or gate of the altar of sacrifice, but John 10:1 says we are considered thieves if we try to skip over Jesus in the Outer Court of our worship.

There are no shortcuts to God's presence; you must go through the door of Jesus. I also want to point out that this outer court represents your flesh, as Jesus came as God in the flesh.

The Shadow of the Inner Court

The inner court was covered under a large tent that actually held both the inner court and inner most court of the tabernacle, divided by a large veil. The first thing you notice when you walk into the Inner Court is that it no longer is lit by the sun. Instead the inner court is lit by seven oil lamps on the lampstand. Oil was constantly maintained in the lamps in order to keep this room lit. The oil represents the power and presence of His Holy Spirit, thus this room represents the Spirit of the Trinity. Now you might think it also represents the spirit in us, but in fact it represents our soul. As we will learn more later, this room is all about the work of the Holy Spirit through our mind, will, and emotions, which is our soul.

The Shadow of the Most Holy Place

In the Most Holy Place, the Ark of the Covenant is the only furniture piece. The Ark of the Covenant was the very place God was thought to dwell in the Old Testament (Exodus 25:22). This room then obviously represents the Father of the trinity. This room was completely blocked from the outside world and its only means of light was the glory of God Himself. Isaiah 60:19 speaks of this glory light. As the Tabernacle ourselves this represents our Spirit where God's presence resides.

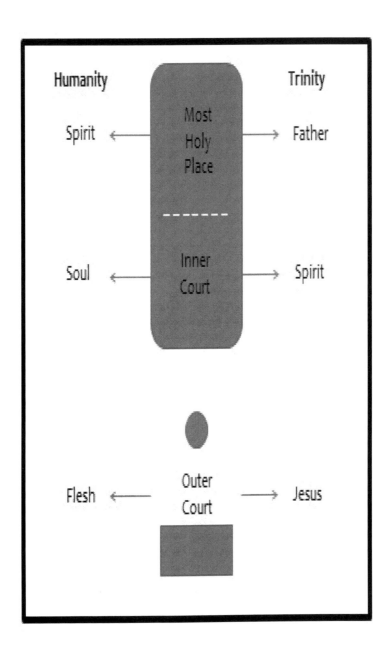

"Jumping Off" Place

In the next six chapters we are going to address each room and place of worship as it pertains to us individually as the tabernacle, and as a family pursing the presence of God.

As we discover revelation and insight as to what transpired in each place of worship, this will become a "jumping off" place for me to share creative ideas your family can use to pursue presence- driven worship.

I have found that most parents want to pursue this type of worship experience with their families, but have no idea how to start. These six places, or postures of worship if you will, will give your family that place to start. Weather you engage in presence- driven worship every night, once a week, or once a month, you can look to the tabernacle and choose a posture of worship for that experience or perhaps even several in one sitting. Either way I believe as you embrace these "jumping off" places within God's steps of worship, the Holy Spirit will take over and continue to give you fresh and new ideas. However, any act of worship I give you can be repeated over and over again as your family goes on this journey together.

I want to lastly encourage you to keep in mind that I could not possibly put every act of worship I have ever done with my family or families within this book. I have, however, written many resources you can purchase that will give you more of them. For your family I would encourage you to look into purchasing our *Stone Moments Family Worship Manual.* It has a total of 72 acts of worship you can engage in with your family. Some are in this book, many are not. We offer many more resources in addition to this one of which all of them have opportunity for presence- driven family worship. All of these resources are highlighted in the back of this book.

The Altar of

Sacrifice

Chapter 9

A Sacrifice Required

The Altar of Burnt Offerings, or the Altar of Sacrifice as it is called, is the very first furniture piece of the Tabernacle of Moses. It is in the Outer Court of the Tabernacle. When God found Adam and Eve, He covered them with animal skin. God needed a way for Adam and Eve's sin to be covered so God could come near them again. In Hebrews 9:22 the bible says. "According to the law almost all things are purified with blood, and without shedding of blood there is no remission of sin." If God was going to be able to enjoy being with His children, they would have to be cleansed and purified in blood. The bible also says in Romans 6:23, "For the wages of sin is death." There was a price to be paid for their sin, and that was death. God loved His children so He established an exchange offering; the animal's death for their life. When God established the Tabernacle of Moses to be the place where He would dwell and be with His children, the very first step was to cover their sins with the blood of animals and to reconcile the judgment of God for sin through the death of an animal. Without this step of worship no man could come close to God.

A Shadow of Christ Revealed

Jesus is not just the Son of God who died on the cross, He is the Lamb of God who shed His blood and died so we didn't have to (John 1:29). The Altar of Sacrifice was a foreshadowing of Christ. The stone altar was simply replaced by a wooden tree in the New Testament.

> *When God ordered the first step of worship in the tabernacle to be at the Altar of Sacrifice, He was simply setting up the scene for our very first act of worship; receiving Jesus as the Lamb of God who takes away our sin, our sickness, and judgement (Isiah 53:5).*

Jesus exchanges His life for ours (Colossians 1:21-22). In Hebrews 10:4 it says, "For it is not possible that the blood of bulls and goats could take away sins." The blood of animals only covered the sin. They had to make a new sacrifice year after year. The blood of animals did not have the power to change the hearts of man, so they would not sin again, but the blood of Jesus, along with the Holy Spirit, has the power to remove sin completely. We are brought back into that holy image of God again through the blood and flesh of Jesus. Through Jesus, "You who once were far off have been brought near by the blood of Christ (Ephesians 2:13)."

The Altar in us

The foreshadowing of the Altar of Sacrifice does not stop with Jesus. Remember, every furniture piece of the Tabernacle of Moses is now in us. We carry the Altar of Sacrifice within us as well. This altar in us represents the death and sacrifice of our flesh as we live through Christ. Jesus said in Luke 9:23 that we must deny ourselves and take up our own cross (altar). Receiving Jesus' death as the Lamb of God ensures us life eternal, and opens the door of supernatural healing and deliverance.

> *But the second most important act of worship you could ever give to God is to lay yourself down on the Altar of Sacrifice and surrender your life, your desires, your will, and heart to Jesus.*

This place of surrender is what brings us close to God's presence again in worship. We are to become living sacrifices (Romans 12:1). In 1 Corinthians 15:31, Paul says he dies daily with Christ. That means, as we wake up every morning, we must decide if we are going to exchange what we want to do or think for what Christ wants to do through us. This is the act of making Jesus not just our savior but our Lord. To make Jesus Lord over your life is to make Him owner of your life. Your life is not your own, it is only through Christ that we can draw near to God. Galatians 2:20 says it like this, "I have been crucified with Christ; it is no longer I who live, but Christ lives in me (Gal 2:20)."

"Jumping Off" Ideas

Family Communion

Things needed: Elements for communion (see details below)

Scripture: 1 Corinthians 11:23-26 and Isiah 53

Music: Choose worship that sets the focus on Jesus, the blood, or the victory of the cross and resurrection.

In this presence-driven family worship experience you are going to focus on family communion. You do not have to have all the official elements to have communion in your home. Simply use crackers or bread of any kind, along with grape juice or any other kind of juice you may have to represent Jesus as the first fruit. You may read from 1 Corinthians 11:23-26 or simply use your own words to go through the worship experience. Allow every family member to have their role in praying and speaking on communion as they wish. Spend time afterwards singing songs together, praying for anyone that is sick, and of course focusing on the presence of God.

Family of Priest

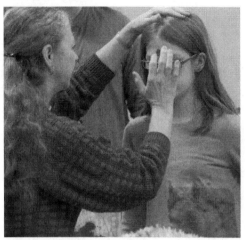

Things Needed: Red paint of any kind. If you have smaller children you might want to make it washable.

Scripture: Exodus 29:20-21

Music: The focus with this act of worship will be simply to set the atmosphere. You may even want to use instrumental music so there is no mix of voices going on.

In this presence-driven family worship experience you are going to focus on anointing your family to become a Priest unto the Lord. As worship music plays, read the above passage of scripture and begin to put the red paint on each family member's right ear, thumb, and toe, calling them to be a Priest unto God. Pray that their ears will hear what God has to say, hands will do what God wants them to do, and feet will go where God wants them to go. Lastly make sure either your spouse or one of your family members does the same over you. Spend time at the end listening for the voice of God as it pertains to your prayer.

Applying the Blood to Your Home

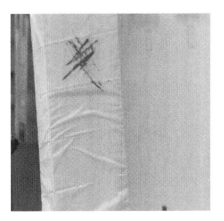

Things Needed: Cardstock or a piece of white plastic table cloth and red paint.

Scripture: Exodus 12:23

Music: If possible, use an IPOD or music player that you can carry from room to room in your house as you enter into this worship exercise. Use music that speaks of the truth and power of His blood.

In this presence-driven family worship experience, you are going to focus on applying the blood of Jesus to your home. Spend some time talking and discussing the power of His blood that still works today. Then with your blood in hand lead the family to every entry door to the house and inside doors applying the anointing oil and declaring Jesus' blood over your home. Use the paper or plastic table cloth to apply the blood on, and then tape it over the doorpost if you do not want permeant marks on your walls or doors. Let each member of the family get a chance to apply the paint. After every doorpost has been marked, worship in victory of what the blood has done for your family.

Sacrificial Offering

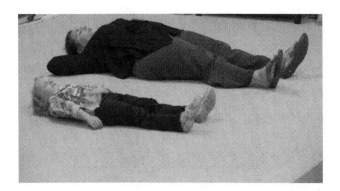

Things Needed: Nothing is needed for this worship time, however if you would like to use any media from the internet to pull up a picture of Jesus on the cross and/or the altar of sacrifice this may give your family a visual to tie the worship together.

Scripture: Galatians 2:20 and Romans 12:1

Music: Use music that focuses on the theme of surrendering to Jesus and yielding to His will in your life. If nothing else, simply use instrumental music again to create an atmosphere.

In this presence-driven family worship experience you are going to focus on presenting yourself as a living sacrifice to the Lord. Encourage each one of your family members to pray a surrendered prayer, helping the little ones. Spend time in His presence, asking Him to reveal anything you need to surrender in your life.

The Bronze Laver

Chapter 10

The Resurrection of Christ

The next step of worship through the tabernacle of Moses is the Bronze Laver. This furniture piece is also in the outer court of the tabernacle. The bronze laver was basically a very large bowl made out of bronze filled with water. The Priest would come over to the wash basin after sacrificing the animal and wash his hands and feet of the blood that had gotten on him during the sacrificial act of worship. This would make them clean and new again. The bible says that this act of worship was so important that if they did not do this step they would die when entering into the holy place (Exodus 30:21). The water of the Bronze Laver is a shadow of the Holy Spirit who brought Jesus back to life (1 Peter 3:18).

We experience Christ's death at the altar of sacrifice, but we experience His life at the bronze laver.

The bronze laver represents the born again experience for us. In fact, when you were born in the natural you were held in your mothers belly by a sack of water, isn't it interesting that there is a bowl of water to represent the born again experience through Christ. Listen to the description of this act of worship in Titus 3:5-6, "according to His mercy He saved us, through the washing of regeneration and renewing of the

Holy Spirit, whom He poured out on us abundantly through Jesus Christ our Savior."

Water Baptism

According to scripture and in the order of the tabernacle, we understand that receiving Christ's death is the very first step of worship, the second step is receiving His life by the Holy Spirit, the third step is being water baptized as a testimony of what you have just done. Romans 6:3 says, "When we are lowered into the water, it is like the burial of Jesus; when we are raised up out of the water, it is like the resurrection of Jesus (MSG)." As the priest would wash with this water removing the stains of death it was as if they were water baptizing themselves as a testimony of Christ's death and resurrection. Water baptism allows us to testify publically that we (our flesh and own will) have been buried with Christ and now we live through Christ. When the priest would wash their hands, water now covered them. This water, representing the Holy Spirit, was the very nature and character of Christ. Galatians 3:26-27 says it this way, "Those who are baptized in the spirit put on Christ."

At the bronze laver is where we choose to participate in the act of worship called water baptism; where we put on Christ. It is our declaration that we are going to become the hands and feet of Christ on earth.

This last step of worship in the Outer Court prepares for the work of Christ in the Inner Court.

Baptism in the Spirit

It takes more than just to be covered in His spirit and looking like Him to do what He did on this earth. The Bible says that we must have the mind of Christ; to think like and act like Jesus. Just as Jesus never did anything He didn't see or hear His father do, we are to do the same. How do we get the heart and mind of Christ? It takes the power of the

Holy Spirit on the inside of us. This is found at the bronze laver in the act of the baptism of the Holy Spirit.

Just as the water in the Laver represents the Holy Spirit, the bronze bowl represents humanity; us in our flesh. God was foreshadowing for us at the bronze laver what He was going to do on the inside of us; fill us with His Holy Spirit.

Let's look at a beautiful picture of worship at the bronze laver through Jesus. Jesus was found in the upper room with His disciples partaking of the last supper. Jesus lead the disciples that night to the Altar of Sacrifice through the partaking of the elements of communion, He then lead them right to the Bronze Laver and washed their feet by the washing of the Spirit. As Jesus washed His disciple's feet however this conversation took place: "What I am doing you do not understand now, but you will know after this (John 13:7)." Peter said to Jesus, "You shall never wash my feet! (John 13:7)", but Jesus answered him, "If I do not wash you, you have no part with Me (John 13:8)." What was the "after this" moment Jesus was talking about you might ask? The Baptism of the Holy Spirit. The disciples were instructed to wait in the upper room for the promise of the father, better known as the baptism of the Holy Spirit, before going to do the work of Jesus, we are to do the same at the Bronze Laver.

The Baptism of the Holy Spirit is the endowment of power, or infilling of power of the Holy Spirit, that enables us to be changed from the inside out and change others to the glory of God.

Jesus said, "He who believes in Me, as the Scripture has said, out of his heart will flow rivers of living water (John 7:37-38)." The water of the Holy Spirit on the inside of you begins to move and pour out through the baptism of the Holy Spirit.

I like to explain it in this away to families. Air is air no matter if it is moving or not. Water is water no matter if it is moving or not. However, when you get air and water moving and stirred up they create power;

kinetic energy. They have the power to move things, to shake things, to change things. The same is with the spirit within us. When we receive Jesus through the baptism of salvation we receive the spirit of God, but when we receive the baptism of the Holy Spirit we are yielded to Him in such a way that He begins to move in us to create power; power to move things, change things, shake things up.

Often the evidence of this power will be receiving a prayer language, or heavenly language, as some people call it. Mark 16:16 speaks of all believers receiving this language. Praying in our prayer language has great benefits. 1 Corinthians 14:4 tells us that our tongues edifies or builds us up in our faith, and 1 Corinthian's 14:2-3 describes it as a language that speaks mysteries directly to God. This is a place of genuine worship, for it is not our flesh at work but our spirit.

"Jumping Off" Ideas

Washing Hands and Feet

Things Needed: A large bowl of water and a towel

Scripture: Psalms 24:3-4 and Galatians 3:26-27

Music: Your focus of music should be around the theme of inviting the Holy Spirit to pour down and to cleanse.

In this presence-driven family worship experience you are going to focus on washing each other's hands and feet. Lead each family member in a cleansing prayer (i.e., "Forgive me, Father, of my sins, by Your Son, Jesus, cleanse my hands and make my heart holy before You.") as you wash their hands in the bowl of water. Pray over them to be clothed in the Holy Spirit, the righteousness of God. Have either your spouse or one of your children to do it for you. Now as Jesus modeled before us, take the time to wash each other's feet to bless each other.

Baptism of the Spirit

Things Needed: Bowl of Water

Scripture: John 7:37-38 and Acts 2

Music: Play music that focuses on the baptism of the Holy Spirit

In this presence-driven family worship experience you are going to focus on the baptism of the Holy Spirit. Have a bowl of water as an object lesson as you discuss the baptism of the Holy Spirit with your family. If anyone does not have it and desires, have your entire family gather around them to receive. Spend some time praying and worshipping with your spirit language as a family. If someone does not have the baptism and the manifestation of receiving it that day does not come, ask them to worship in their own language of understanding.

Soaking in the Spirit

Things Needed: Large bowl of warm water for each person in your family

Scripture: Psalms 46:10, Galatians 3:26-27, and Acts 2:17

Music: This is a perfect time just to play instrumental Music and set the atmosphere for the Holy Spirit to minister.

In this presence-driven family worship experience you are going to focus on feeling the presence of God. As you discuss the scriptures compare the water of a bath with the water of the Spirit. Encourage everyone to place their feet in their warm bowl of water having everyone share how it feels to be emerged in the water liken to the spirit. Allow the presence of God to come in and have everyone pay close to attention to what it feels like to be in the presence of God in that moment. Perhaps some may begin to pray in their heavenly language, others may be quite full of peace, others full of joy or crying.

The Lampstand

Chapter 11

The Light that Brings Repentance

We are going to move from the outer court into the inner court of the tabernacle of Moses. This room focuses on the Holy Spirit of the Trinity and is about the work of ministry in us and through us. The Lampstand was the furniture piece that lit this whole room up. It was fueled with oil. As we talked about it briefly previously, the oil represents Holy Spirit. The Holy Spirit has many jobs on this earth.

One of the jobs of the Holy Spirit is foreshadowed at the Lampstand; to uncover or bring light to the hidden things of our hearts.

Proverbs 20:27 says, "The spirit of a man is the lamp of the LORD, Searching all the inner depths of his heart." This is what David was asking for in Psalms 139:23 when he asked God to search him. The Holy Spirit comes into our hearts with His light, the truth of God, and shines it into the dark places of our soul revealing to us sin and thoughts that are not of God. Why is this act of worship important? So that we may repent, change the way we think, into the mind of Christ. This act of worship that leads us to repentance must be done in order for us to be in the presence of God's holiness and to become like His son Jesus.

The Light that Brings Revelation

The second foreshadow of the lampstand in us is the Holy Spirit bringing us into revelation of who God is and what His word means. Revelation means to be brought into more of a full understanding of something that you previously knew a little about.

Many religious leaders and Israelites of Jesus' day saw Jesus; they heard Him speak, they saw Him perform miracles, but they did not have a revelation of who Jesus truly was; they only saw Jesus in part.

But Jesus asked Peter, "But who do you say that I am (Matthew 16:15)?" Simon Peter answered and said, "You are the Christ, the Son of the living God." Jesus answered and said to him, "Blessed are you, Simon Bar-Jonah, for flesh and blood has not revealed this to you, but My Father who is in heaven (Matt 16:17)." The Spirit of God had revealed who Jesus was to Peter. The light of the Holy Spirit illuminates hidden things within God's word and Kingdom to reveal to us deeper revelation of who He is and who we are to Him. The Bible calls these hidden things "mysteries". Jesus says in Luke 8:10 that as children of God, the Holy Spirit will reveal to us the mysteries of God and His kingdom. When we worship God at the lampstand we are allowing the light of the Holy Spirit to reveal these mysteries.

Being the Light

Remember the inner court room is not only about the work of the Holy Spirit in us, but it is about the work of the Holy Spirit through us.

> *"You are the light of the world. A city that is set on a hill cannot be hidden. "Nor do they light a lamp and put it under a basket, but on a lampstand, and it gives light to all who are in the house." Let your light so shine before men, that they may see your good works and glorify your Father in heaven." Matt 5:14-16*

These are the words of Jesus to us. Isn't it interesting that He would use the very word lampstand in this scripture as He tells us that we are the light to the world? So how do we become the light to the world? Jesus tells us, "that they may see your good works." The last act of worship at the lampstand of the tabernacle for our families is to go and do for others. The light of the Holy Spirit on the inside of us, changes us into the nature and character of Jesus. He then gives us the very power we need to share that light with others around us. We share our light within us by what we do and say to our neighbors, our friends, family, and community. We let the lampstand within us shine for others to see until they can't help but to repent and want what we have.

"Jumping Off" Ideas

Revealing Light

Things Needed: Small clay pots (one for each person, permeant markers, hammer, and a plastic table cloth

Scripture: Provers 20:27 and Psalms 139:23

Music: I would encourage you to start out with instrumental music allowing no distractions to hearing God's voice. Then as you move into your pot crushing exercise, use victory worship songs cheering each person on.

In this presence-driven family worship experience you are going to focus on allowing the Holy Spirit to reveal things in your heart that are not of God. Have everyone either stand, sit, or lay down quietly listening for the voice of the Holy Spirit to bring anything to light that He wants us to remove from our hearts. Instruct each person to write that down on their clay pot. After everyone is done, one at a time share what you wrote on your clay pot and break it as a sign of repentance and removal of those things.

Revelation of the Word

What's Needed: Candle for each person, a Bible, and a piece of paper to write on for each family member

Scripture: Luke 8:10

Music: You will want to use instrumental music for this worship experience creating an atmosphere of the presence of God.

In this presence-driven family worship experience, you are going to focus on receiving revelation of God's word. Each person will choose a place in the room, light their candle and place it near them on a table, and choose one passage of scripture that they want to read quietly to themselves. Instruct them that after they read it, they are going to ask the light of the Holy Spirit to reveal anything God has hidden in that passage as a mystery. They will then read again searching for the mysteries and writing down anything they find. Spend time to share as a family afterwards.

Go and Be the Light

Things' Needed: Piece of paper to write on

Scripture: Matthew 5:14-16

Music: Use instrumental to set the atmosphere for the Holy Spirit to speak to each person

In this presence-driven family worship experience you are going to focus on being the light outside your house. My favorite way to reach out is what is known as *treasure hunting.* Plan to take your family to the park, mall, even in your local neighborhood to pray for those who God highlights to you. Here is how it works. As a family spend some time with the Holy Spirit right before your planned family outreach. Ask the Lord to reveal "hints" or "treasures" to each family member writing them down on your piece of paper. These hints, or treasures, might be something like brown hair, walking dog, woman with red jacket, etc. When you go out you are going to look specifically for these hints as Jesus highlights for you who he wants you to share your light with. It is a very prophetic and spirit-driven way to do an outreach.

The Table of Showbread

Chapter 12

Collecting the Bread

From the Lampstand, directly across the room is called the Table of Showbread. It was simply a table that the priest would display the bread and grain offerings from the people (exodus 25:23). To begin to explore the foreshadowing revealed at this table, we must look at a story in the Bible found in Exodus 16. The Israelites were stuck in the wilderness, tired and hungry. They had already forgotten the promise of God to bring them into a land filled with milk and honey. So the Bible says that God heard their complaints and rained down bread from heaven for them to eat every day. Exodus 16:31 says it was like coriander seed and tasted like honey. The interesting thing about this seed is that it is white like milk and it tasted like honey which sounds a lot like their promise from God to be given a land filled with milk and honey (Exodus 3:8). So, at first glance we can see how the bread on the table of showbread spiritually was a reminder of the promises of God.

Today we don't have bread raining down from heaven, but what we do have to eat to remind us of the promises of God, is the word of God.

God instructed the Israelites to collect this bread daily; not just once a week or in church. In fact if they tried to skip a day and eat off of yesterday's bread it would get moldy. We must be reminded of God's promises for us every day.

Eating the Bread

The bread was not just collected, it was eaten. Jesus said when rebuking the devil in the wilderness, "Man shall not live by bread alone, but by every word that proceeds from the mouth of God (Matthew 4:4)."

Our natural bodies need food to eat, but spiritually we need God's word just as much. Our spirits will die without constantly being nourished by God's word.

God beckons us to, "Taste and see that the Lord is good, Blessed be the man who trusts in Him (Psalms 34:8)." God is asking us to eat His word and see if it is not good... we must trust Him. God commanded Ezekiel to eat the scroll of God, God's word, so that he would not just collect God's word, but that it would become a part of him (Ezekiel 3:1). You see, it is easy to read the Bible and memorize a scripture or two, but unless you get the words of God inside of you, it will never be a part of who you are; you will not ever believe it. God says in Isaiah 55:10 that His word is like seed that is planted and produces the fruit that he said it was going to. When we eat God's word it becomes not just something we know, but something we GROW. Mixing what we read with the presence of the Spirit enables the Holy Spirit to take it from our minds to our spirits. This makes that old phrase "You are what you eat" true in our lives!

Speaking the Promise

The problem the Israelites had in the wilderness is they complained too much. Even though they knew what God had really done for them they spoke something very different. They chose to speak the opposite of what they just had eaten. They should have been saying how good God is, how sweet He is. Instead, they complained for forty years in the wilderness and most died before ever seeing the promise land. The Bible says in Proverbs 18:21, "Death and life are in the power of the tongue, and those who love it will eat its fruit." This means that whatever we say has the power to produce that in our lives or other people's lives.

God has given us His promises, He desires us to eat them, and then we must speak them into existence.

If I simply plant a seed in soil, will it grow into a sunflower? You must give the seed water and sunlight. When we mix reading God's word with the Spirit, we water the seed. But when we begin to speak it, we release it into the light of Jesus allowing full growth of the promise of God on the inside of us to produce its fruit. Psalms 71:24 says, "My tongue also shall talk of Your righteousness all the day long." Speaking, praying, and singing the word of God is the last step of worship at the Table of Showbread; we do this for ourselves and in ministry to others.

"Jumping Off" Ideas

Promises of the Word

Things Needed: Coriander Seed, Bible, and bread

Scripture: Exodus 16:31 and Exodus 3:8

Music: Set the atmosphere for the presence of God through quiet worship music that focuses on the promises of God for believers.

In this presence-driven family worship experience for your family you are going to focus on the promises of God in His word. Show your family what coriander seed looks like as you discuss the scriptures? Next you're going to find some promises of God in His word. There are many resources you can use online by googling the promises of God in the Bible, promise scriptures, etc. This will give you a starting point. You can also sit down and simply ask everyone to give you a promise they know from the word, and then search where it is in the Bible. After having your scriptures, look them up and take turns reading them out loud and thanking Jesus for His promises in His word. Eat bread together as you continue to worship the Lord.

Daily Bread

Things Needed: Bible and Bread

Scripture: Matthew 4:4, Ezekiel 3:1, and Isaiah 55:10

Music: you will be setting the atmosphere for the presence of God. It needs to be soft worship music or instrumental.

For this presence-driven family worship experience, you are going to focus reading the Word daily. Pick a passage of scripture to read from as a family. As each member of the family takes a turn reading a verse, they get to eat a piece of bread. Discuss in the end what the passage means and pray that it begins to be a seed planted in each one of you. Encourage your family to read the word daily.

Speaking Life

Things Needed: Bible and Bread

Scripture: Proverbs 18:21 and Psalms 71:24

Music: Create an atmosphere of the presence of God with soft worship music

In this presence-driven family worship experience you will focus on declaring God's word. You're going to find some promises of God in His word. There are many resources you can use online by googling the promises of God in the Bible, promise scriptures, etc. This will give you a starting point. You can also set down and simply ask everyone to give you a promise they know from the Word, then search where that is in the Bible. Each person is to pick a promise and a member of the family to pray and declare that word over.

The Altar of

Incense

Chapter 13

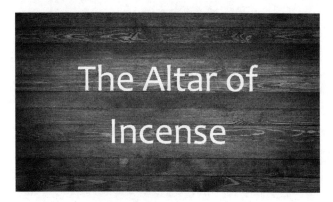

The Scent of Our Worship

The last step of worship before entering into the Inner Most Court is the Altar of Incense. The Altar of Incense is where the priest was required to burn incense day and night (Exodus 30:7-8). Ephesians 5:2 tells us, "walk in love, as Christ also has loved us and given Himself for us, an offering and a sacrifice to God for a sweet-smelling aroma." When we express God's love that is worship, and that worship has the power to create an aroma.

> *A scent of something can make you feel good or it can make you feel bad. Our worship has the same power with God.*

God said in Isaiah 1:13, "Bring no more futile sacrifices; Incense is an abomination to Me." Worship that does not come from the heart is foul smelling to God. Luke 10:27 says, "You shall love the LORD your God with all your heart, with all your soul, with all your strength, and with all your mind and 'your neighbor as yourself." Our worship to God must be to give all of our self, that is why this is called an altar; a sacrifice unto the Lord. The incense was to burn continually, which is a picture of how we are to have a lifestyle of worship unto God.

The Cloud of God's Presence

As incense was burned, a cloud of smoke would bellow out from it. This smoke is a foreshadowing of God's presence. God said to the Israelites, "And the LORD went before them by day in a pillar of cloud to lead the way (Exodus 13:21)." James 4:8 says that as we draw near to God He draws near to us. This means as we worship it produces God presence; the Holy Spirit. As we lift up our hands, sing praises to Him, as we share God's love with others, as we obey His word, His presence comes down and lifts our worship up to God.

The scent of our worship is mixed with the cloud of His presence and is offered up before God.

We don't see clouds as evidence of God's presence today like the Israelites did in the wilderness. However we can see, feel, and even hear the evidence of the presence of God in our lives in many ways. The first way is by feeling and giving love. God is love so it is impossible to feel Godly love or give Godly love without His presence. Some people describe feeling God's love as if a warm blanket were wrapped around them, as rushing water covering them, or rushing wind, or through peace, joy, power, gifts of the spirit, and many more because these are the very characteristics of the Holy Spirit.

Loving Others through Our Worship

The last thing we are going to explore at the Altar of Incense is how we serve others at this place of worship. We mentioned earlier Luke 10:27, "You shall love the LORD your God with all your heart, with all your soul, with all your strength, and with all your mind,' and 'your neighbor as yourself." Not only does this scripture tell us to love God with all that we are, but it tells us that we must love others. Worship is not only expressing our love to God, it is expressing God's love to others.

104

Psalms 141:2 says, "Let my prayer be set before You as incense, The lifting up of my hands as the evening sacrifice". The Altar of Incense is where we get to worship God through intercession; prayers for others."

Intercession simply is when we stand between a person and heaven and pray for them. It is also called standing in the gap for someone. Just as our praise goes up before God through the smoke/cloud of His presence, so does our prayers. In fact, the most effective prayers we can pray is in the midst of worship and the presence of God, because it is through the spirit we can pray God's will for someone. In revelation 8:3-5 it says that your prayers are captured by the angels and presented before God, and when the time comes to answer that prayer, it is thrown to the earth with thunder and lightning.

"Jumping Off" Ideas

Producing the Cloud

Things Needed: Incense to burn

Scripture: Isiah 1:13, Luke 10:27 and James 4:8

Music: This is one of the few times I would encourage you to find anointed and presence filled worship songs that your whole family knows and understands the words.

In this presence-filled family worship experience you will focus on worshipping with all your heart, soul, and mind to the Lord offering a sweet aroma and the presence of God. Again, this is one of those rare worship experiences that is focused on singing songs as a family but certainly not limited to. If the Lord leads, create spontaneous worship songs to the Lord in your time as well. Burn the incense during worship as a reminder of what our worship produces to the Lord.

Intercession for Each Other

Things Needed: Chair positioned in the center of the room

Scripture: psalms 141:2

Music: Anointed worship music focused on who God is and what He has done for us at the cross.

This presence-driven family worship experience will focus on praying one for another. You will want to start out simply worshipping as a family to draw in the presence of God for a time. Then one at a time have someone sit in the "hot seat" while everyone else prays for them out-loud. If there is a particular prayer request, let that person share before prayers are offered up.

Building a Moment

Things Needed: building Blocks of any kind

Scripture: Acts 10:4 and Revelations 8:3-5

Music: Use quite worship or instrumental music

In this presence-driven family worship experience you will focus on intercession for others outside of your home (i.e. church, city, state, nation, nations, etc.). Talk about how Cornelius' prayers went up before the Lord and made a memorial. A memorial is to remember what has happened. God remembered Cornelius's prayer and answered them. Show your family the pictures of the national memorials and what they help us remember. As you begin to worship the Lord, focus your prayers for anyone or anything outside of your home. As each person says a prayer, they get to add a block, making memorial before the Lord.

The Ark of the
Covenant

Chapter 14

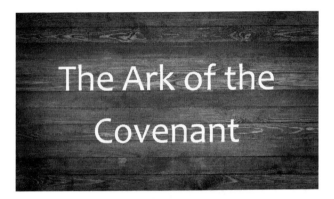

The Fullness of God's Presence

Now we are ready to step into the room in the Inner Most Court where the Ark of the Covenant or the ark of testimony is. In this room, inside the box of the ark was where the holy presence of God was contained. The high priest of Moses' day was only able to come into this room, separated by a veil, one day a year where he was commanded to bring in the blood of a sacrifice and incense from the altar of worship (Leviticus 16:11-14).

> *Today as priests unto God, our spirits have become the very dwelling place of God, meaning we have become that room and ark, twenty four-seven.*

The bible says, "Therefore, brethren, having boldness to enter the Holiest by the blood of Jesus, by a new and living way which He consecrated for us, through the veil, that is, His flesh (Hebrew 10:19-20)." Today there is still a veil we must go through; the blood of the Lamb of God that we received at the altar of sacrifice. And guess what, we still need the incense which produces the Holy Spirit found at the altar of our worship. There are no shortcuts to get to God, but when we finally step into that room both Father (within the Ark), Son (the blood of Jesus we received at the Altar of Sacrifice), and Holy Spirit (represented through the Altar of Incense) are represented; the fullness of who God is. It is through Jesus and our worship that we get to be in the presence of a Holy God.

The Power of God's Presence

In the Most Holy place is where we do nothing and God does everything. In the outer and inner court something was required of us, but once we step into this room, God does all the work and we simply receive.

In 1 Kings 8:11, this is what happened to the priest as the cloud of God's glory filled the tent. In exodus 24:17 it says, "The sight of the glory of the LORD was like a consuming fire." Remember, the very glory of God, His holiness and righteousness, is what lights up the room of the most holy place. This light of holiness was a fire that would burn out anything not holy that it touched. This all-consuming fire of God is also used to burn up or destroy our enemy (Deuteronomy 9:3). If you stand still in His presence, you allow God to fight your battles for you. These truths should lead us to have a holy fear of God; a fear of reverence and respect for who God is and the power He holds in our lives. As long as we come to God under the blood of His son we will not physically die, but our sin dies. The more we step into the most holy place with God, the more we become holy, sanctified, and safe from our enemies. This understanding and honor to whom God is and what He can do is called the fear of the Lord.

The Life is in God's Presence

It is thought that the glory of the Lord rests in between the wings of the angels on top of the Ark of the Covenant. As His glory shined, it would cast a shadow off the angels. This gives us a clear picture as to what Psalms 91:1 means when it says,

"He who dwells in the secret place of the Most High shall abide under the shadow of the Almighty."

We abide, which means to rest or be with, right in God's glory under the wings. Who has ever felt like hiding from a rough day or from a trial or tribulation? In Psalms 16:11, it says we find joy and pleasure in His presence. We also feel His love, for God is love. We also find life in His presence. In the Old Testament, Aarons' rod, which is in the Ark of the Covenant, was actually a dead almond branch and as it lay in God's glory in the most holy place it began to bud and come back to life. Malachi 4:2 says we find healing in His wings. Lastly, it is the place where God speaks to you. "There I will meet with you, and I will speak with you from above the mercy seat, from between the two cherubim which are on the Ark of the Testimony (Exodus 25:22)." God desires to not just to be with His children, He desires to speak to His children. It is really hard to hear what someone is saying when you're the one doing the ministering, the praying, and the work. In the place of God's glory, we become still and listen for God to speak to us.

"Jumping Off" Ideas

Consuming Fire

Things Needed: fireplace, bon fire, or large candle, and a piece of paper to write on

Scripture: Exodus 24:17 and Deuteronomy 9:3

Music: Your music will set the atmosphere for God's Holy Fire to come

In this presence-driven family worship experience you will focus on God's fire that burns and destroys our enemy. Use the music that focuses on God's holy fire. As you discuss the above scriptures, have everyone begin to share some ways the enemy has attacked them. Maybe through bullying or lies he has spoken to them; maybe it's a trial and tribulation your family has been going through. Have each person write those things down on a piece of paper and as you continue to worship, one at a time place the paper in the fire and declare God's holy fire to destroy it in your life and family. If your fire has to be with a large candle, I recommend placing it in the kitchen sink so that you have water if things get out of hand and everything stays contained.

Fire of Power

Things Needed: Large Candle and a smaller candle for each member of the family

Scripture: Acts 2:3 and Hebrews 12:29

Music: Use anointed worship music that focuses on God's holy fire in us

In this presence-driven family worship experience you will focus on receiving the power of God. Light your candle as you talk about the above scriptures. Discuss with your family what the disciples did after they received fire from God (they saved and healed people). Begin to worship as a family with the music, asking God to send His fire that you may use it to save and heal people. Take the smaller candles and have every member of the family use the larger candle to light their own.

Rest and Listen

Things Needed: large candle or many little ones to light up a room and blanket

Scriptures: Exodus 25:22 and Psalms 91:1

Music: Soaking instrumental worship music that brings God's presence and gives opportunity for the Lord to speak

In this presence-driven family worship experience you will focus on resting in God's holy presence and hearing His voice. Light your candles and turn off all other lights. Have your family lay under a blanket together as you begin to listen to the worship music and rest in the presence of God. Each person should close their eyes and listen for God to speak to them. Afterwards, take time to share what you felt and heard.

The Blueprint for Presence-Driven Family Worship in the Tabernacle

The Ark of the Covenant

The place of God's very character and nature imparted to us. This is where He speaks to us and we rest in His presence

The Altar of Incense

The place where the cloud of His presence in worship and intercession mix to bring a sweet aroma to the Lord.

The Lampstand

The place where the Holy Spirit illuminates are hearts and anoints us to the work of

The Table of Showbread

The place we eat God's word daily and allow the seed to grow and be watered by His presence

Bronze Laver

The place we are washed in Jesus' life and resurrection receiving the baptism of the Holy Spirit

The Altar of Sacrifice

The place we receive Jesus' sacrifice as the Lamb of God and where we become a living sacrifice

Journey Begins

Chapter 15

Your Journey Begins

As I come to the final pages of this book, I realize that my journey with you will have its end soon, but your journey into presence-driven family worship is only beginning. I wanted to leave you with some final thoughts of what to expect in the days ahead, and some encouraging words to help you press on and through any bumps in the road.

God's Grace is Sufficient

You will find that your experience will sometimes be filled with the presence of God where everything is going smoothly and as you had planned. However, there will be other days... well not so much. The reality is that as soon as you start pursuing this type of ministry with your family, the devil is going to be all over you like a bee is to pollen. He is going to understand what a threat you are becoming to his kingdom of darkness and will try everything he can to frustrate and distract you in doing what God has called you to do with your family. I want you to be of good courage that God assures you in 2 Corinthians 12:9, that His "grace is sufficient for you, for My strength is made perfect in weakness." Rest in that. You will have good and bad days. Learn to be content in God's grace that does what you cannot. Count all efforts, no matter how much it seemed they failed, as seed planted;

nothing is wasted in God's kingdom. It is amazing how if we just do our part, taking time out to pursue God's presence through worship as a family, He will do the rest. He honors every effort you put into it.

How Often?

Don't beat yourself up over getting as much time in for presence-driven family worship as possible. Focus on not so much the amount of time as much as the quality of time. If you can't seem to get your family together to worship in His presence more than once a month, let it be once a month. The important thing is to schedule it, put it on your calendar, and do not allow distractions or conflicts to trump this family time. Make it as much as a priority as school, work, and church.

Does Age Matter?

The younger the kids, the more of a challenge family worship experiences will be. There is no magical age to have your kids start engaging in this type of worship. What I have found works best is allowing kids to grow up in it. Let me explain further.

If your kids are toddlers or preschool age, allow the experience to be for you and your spouse. If you are single or your spouse at this point doesn't desire to join in for any reason, then prepare a worship experience for yourself. However, keep an element of inclusion for your child by having them stay in the same room playing quietly. Explain what you are doing and invite them to engage at any time. But be sure to let them know it is quiet playtime if they do not desire to join you. They may go back and forth between play and worship; at this age that is okay. You will be surprised how much they will be effected by watching and listening to what you are doing coupled by the presence of God that will saturate the room. As they mature and grow both spiritually and by age, you will find they will want to be involved and will pick up and start mimicking some of the things you are doing.

If your kids are older, let's say from 6 years and up, and they have not already been introduced to these experiences, they may not desire to engage but they should be required to join in. Depending on their spiritual level though, kids will respond differently and have different levels of engagement. I always say if a child refuses to engage they must stay with the family but not disturb what is going on. You and your spouse are the headship of the home. If you honor the Lord's desire and calling for your family above your child's carnal nature, He will change their heart in time.

The ideal situation however, is to allow your kids to start growing into these family worship times from the toddler years and a lot of the future battles can be avoided.

Family Ministry is Messy:

I want to also forewarn you that family ministry is messy. It is not a neat and organized service like we have in our churches. There is all kinds of distractions that get in the middle of ministry at home, from phone calls to dogs, yes I said dogs. Let me tell you a story of one of my own family messy worship experiences. We had put on slow deep soaking worship music. We had talked about the comparison between soaking in the presence of Jesus and soaking in warm bath water. We each had a large bowl of water we were soaking our feet in as we closed our eyes and rested in the presence of God. Suddenly our dog came prancing into the room and begin to lap up water from each one of our bowls. The kids begin to laugh uncontrollably and any hope of regaining the solemn moment in the presence of God was out the window. However, we will never forget what happened. Life's messy moments of worship somehow can be just a special and memorable than any other time. Learn to roll with it!

The Wow Moment:

If you are consistent with your efforts, there will come a time where you receive that "wow" moment. As parents, we often time wonder if what we are saying and teaching our child will ever produce good fruit in their life. And when it comes to pursuing presence-driven family worship experiences, it is no different. There may be times you wonder if you are ever going to see your reward. Press on and have faith. Hebrews 11:6 says, "He is a rewarder of those who diligently seek Him." Your reward is coming and it will be a wow moment!

I want to leave you with this final personal testimony of my own "wow" moment in my family. Recently a Christian movie came out called **"War Room"**. Our family went to see it but we left our six year old with a babysitter because we were unsure if the content would be okay for her. When the movie came out on DVD, we allowed her to watch it with us in our home. After the movie ended she disappeared to play, so I thought, and I went about my chores of the day. A couple of hours went by and I had not seen her. I went upstairs to her room to find her with the door closed, worshipping with music from her I-POD, praying in the spirit, and writing and taping prayers all over her door. She had, with no prompting from us and no conversation about the movie, went up into her room and established a "War Room." It was just her and the Holy Spirit up there for hours. She is only six! Had she not grown up in a family of presence-driven worshippers she would have not been sensitive to the Holy Spirit's drawing and responded to it. It was my "wow" moment!

 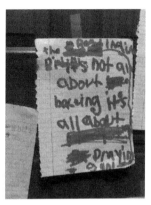

(Isabella's "War Room" filled with prayers and conversation between her and Jesus)

My prayer is that the words written in this book will find itself as truth from the Holy Spirit planted deep within your heart; that you will find yourself saying yes to the calling of the Lord for you as a parent and leader of your family. I pray that this spiritual calling will drive you in every aspect of your life and supersede all others. I also pray God's highest blessing, favor, anointing, and presence upon your home and family as you begin your journey into presence-driven family worship. May you see the fruit of your labor in your children's' lives and their children's children and be used mightily to expand the Kingdom of Heaven on this earth. Let the journey begin!

Family Resources Recommended

Stone Moments Family Manual $12.50

I highly recommended purchasing this resource for your family which will help you continue your journey in presence-driven family worship. It has 72 creative spirit lead acts of worship you can do with your family.

Act of Worship $65.00

This resource although written as a church curriculum, is an excellent resource for home. All 52 acts of worship in this curriculum are in the Stone Moments Manual but in this resource each one comes with a full teaching for your family. This resource covers the acts of worship from simply raising of your hands, knelling, clapping, and singing, to more of the deeper worship like praying in the spirit and listening for the voice of God.

Radical Worship Family Devotional $30.00

Your family will go on a 52 day journey of worship from before the earth was created, to the Garden of Eden, through the Tabernacle of Moses, to the Garden of Gethsemane with Jesus, right to Mary's alabaster box. The Tabernacle teaching in this book came straight out of the pages of this devotional to be shared as a family with discussion questions and presence-driven family worship exercises.

Living Stones Family Devotional $30.00

Through a detailed word study of how God has chosen to use stones in the "seen" world, a picture begins to form that reveals who we are as living stones in the "unseen" world according to 1 Peter 2:4. Your family will take a 40 day journey from the Old Testament to the New, discovering mysteries hidden in God's word to find your calling as Living Stones. This devotional is filled with creative spirit lead worship activities that go along with each subject learned.

Kingdom Family Devotional $30.00

This resource is full of 84 days your family can experience learning about our King and the Kingdom of Heaven together. Through the view finder of a kingdom, they will discover their own purpose for being born on this earth and feel a since of belonging to something greater than themselves. Spirit filled acts of worship is all included in this resources for your family as it pertains to the subject.

Amazing Grace Family Devotional $30.00

This 52 day devotional is all about helping your family find Biblical authentic grace. This resource brings a holistic view of grace that encompasses a foundation of grace based upon a biblical perspective of who God is, who we are not, why we need grace through Christ, the right posture to receive grace, and what the work of grace produces in every believer and family that is yielded to the Holy Spirit. There are opportunities given for presence-driven family worship in the devotional as well.

About Our Ministry to Kids and Families

Chosen Stones Ministries

Chosen Stones Ministries is a focused spirit lead and spirit empowered ministry to families; teaching families how to live and walk by the spirit of God and how to worship in spirit and in truth making worship a lifestyle not a place they go.

We host monthly presence-driven family worship gatherings that engage all ages of the family young and old alike. In these gatherings we train families how to worship together and make a habituation place for the Holy Spirit through modeling and facilitating what we call "acts of Worship". These acts of worship often time use object lessons like communion, laying on of hands, studying and discussing scripture, praying scripture, listening for the voice of God, and using the gifts of the Spirit, all within the paradigm of the family.

It is our desire that the church at large grab hold of our vision for families and begin to host their own presence-driven family worship gatherings. As we equip the families of God to live a lifestyle of worship and create an altar for His presence within their home, our churches will become stronger, more spiritually mature, and filled with the presence of God. It starts in the home!

I currently write presence driven family devotionals for families, host yearly training conferences that include parents, and accept invitations to come to churches to train leaders and parents, and family conferences

Alicia White, founder and Director of Chosen Stones Ministries

www.chosenstones.org, more information: info@chosenstones.org

Kids in Ministry international Ohio

Kids in Ministry International Ohio is a sister ministry to Kids in Ministry int., founded and directed by Becky Fischer in North Dakota. We carry Becky's heart and vision here in Ohio to take the children of God beyond the limitations of man and allow the Holy Spirit, which has no limitations of age, to take over their lives. Far too many years we have held the umbrella of expectation too low for our children in the body, the result being boredom and a mass exodus of children leaving the church when they turn 18 never to return again. It is time that our children experience authentic relationship with Jesus through a spirit-driven life and heavenly supernatural invasions that empower them to do the work of ministry in these last days.

Children can and will experience the tangible presence of God and receive and use the gifts of the Holy Spirit if we allow them opportunity to do so. "Church as usual" will not satisfy this supernatural reality TV generation of the present age. God is pouring down the promise of the Father, "and it shall come to pass in the last days, says God, that I will pour out my spirit on all flesh; your sons and your daughters shall prophesy" (Acts 2:17, NKJV).

At KIMIOhio It is our purpose to train children's leaders how to step out of the box of religion and tradition and embrace teaching children the meat of God's word, activate them in the gifts, and bring them into an encounter with the presence of God on a weekly bases in our churches. We host annual training conferences, revival services, and kid's and family conferences. We offer the **School of the Supernatural** and **PowerClub** training for leaders and parents, and many curriculum resources for children's leaders to use to help them facilitate this vision in their ministry. We also accept invites to come host an event in churches of Ohio.

Alicia White, Ohio Director of Kids in Ministry International Ohio

www.kimiohio.org, more information: kimiohio@ymail.org

Made in the USA
Charleston, SC
15 December 2016